D1107816

DOWN, PEACOCK'S FEATHERS

DOWN, PEACOCK'S FEATHERS

*Studies in the contemporary
significance of the
General Confession*

by
D. R. DAVIES

Revised Edition

*New York
The Macmillan Company
1961*

BX
5145
A633
D3
1961

Revised Edition © Ruth Davies 1961

All rights reserved—no part of this book may be reproduced in any form without permission in writing from the publisher, except by a reviewer who wishes to quote brief passages in connection with a review written for inclusion in magazine or newspaper.

First Printing

Printed in the United States of America

Library of Congress catalog card number: 61-10342

TO
ALEC R. VIDLER
An Uncompromising Churchman
and a Faithful Friend

50715

"Wherefore, good people, let us beware of such hypocrisy, vain-glory, and justifying of ourselves. Let us look upon our feet; and then down peacock's feathers, down proud heart, down vile clay, frail and brittle vessels."

"The Misery of Man" in *Book of Homilies*

50715

NOTE

THIS BOOK, FIRST WRITTEN DURING THE LAST WAR, was so much esteemed that it had to be reprinted a number of times, but it has long been out of print. My husband intended to rewrite it, but death overtook him before he could get the work ready for the press. A friend who wishes to remain anonymous has done this service for him, confident that many in this country and abroad will be glad to have the results of his maturer thoughts. He said more than once: "This is my Testament", and my hope is that the book as it now stands will be received as the last words of one who died in the service of the Church and was a highly regarded teacher.

When this book was first published a number of readers wrote to my husband to say that they could not find the phrase "Down Peacock's Feathers" in the Book of Homilies. The fact is that the passage containing this expression was in the original but was for some reason omitted from many later editions. For details, see *Theology*, January, 1952, pp. 26 ff.

DECEMBER 1960   RUTH DAVIES

AUTHOR'S PREFACE TO THE
FIRST EDITION OF 1942

AFTER I WAS CONFIRMED BY THE BISHOP OF ST.
Asaph, and began to repeat the Offices of the Prayer
Book daily, I was very deeply struck by the General
Confession. Its painful relevance to the existing situation of the world forced itself upon my mind. I then
looked about for a book on the General Confession,
but in the magnificent Library of St. Deiniol's,
Hawarden—a library of 60,000 volumes, *there was not
a single book devoted to the General Confession.* And I
was informed, on excellent authority, that there is not
one book in Anglican theology written exclusively
on it. Neither have I yet come across anyone among
my Anglican friends, either clerical or lay, who knows
of one. It is clear, in any case, that there is a great dearth
of literature dealing with the General Confession.
This seems to me, a recent convert to Anglicanism,
an astonishing neglect. If there was ever a scripture,
outside the Canon, that bore the marks of the Holy
Ghost, the General Confession can certainly claim to
be that scripture.

So I am in what must be a very rare and happy
situation for an author; I am not under necessity to
apologise for adding another book to an already
existing voluminous literature. Even if I am not the

very first to tread virgin soil, the footmarks of my pre-
decessors, if any, are so few and faint that any apology
due is to the General Confession for an amazingly
belated exploration. The fact that I am a newcomer
to the Anglican Church may not be altogether a dis-
advantage. If belief constitutes a qualification, then I
am well qualified to write a commentary on the
General Confession; for I believe its truth absolutely.
Especially do I subscribe to its more offensive clauses—
offensive, that is, to the modern, progressive mind.
I have heard more than one Churchman say that the
one thing he wouldn't accept in the General Confession
was its affirmation that "there is no health in us". As
the reader will see, that is the part which I believe
with the utmost conviction. I am all for clouting the
secularised mind—hard. The General Confession is a
magnificent sledge-hammer!

So, as a stimulus to other Anglican thinkers, better
equipped than myself, I am offering this study of the
General Confession, in the hope that they will go one
better. I am offering it as *a serious sociological hypothesis*
in a time of disillusionment and confusion. Perhaps
today, the sociology of the Confession is temporarily
of greater significance than its theology—which is
permanently important.

This preface would outrun Mr. Bernard Shaw's
prefaces in length, if I were to begin to acknowledge
my obligations. The informed reader will have little
difficulty in recognising them. But I must express my
gratitude to Father Vidler for the title of the book. He

made a handsome present of it to me. Even if the reader will not like the book, I hope he will like the title. I unashamedly think it's a gorgeous title. My thanks are also due to the Oxford University Press for permission to quote the long extract from their publication of Theodore Haecker's *Søren Kierkegaard*, and to the S.C.M. Press for permission to quote from their publication of Dr. Arnold Toynbee's *Christianity and Civilization*.

D. R. DAVIES

HULL

THE GENERAL CONFESSION

Almighty and most merciful Father; We have erred, and strayed from thy ways like lost sheep. We have followed too much the devices and desires of our own hearts. We have offended against thy holy laws. We have left undone those things which we ought to have done; And we have done those things which we ought not to have done; And there is no health in us. But thou, O Lord, have mercy upon us, miserable offenders. Spare thou them, O God, which confess their faults. Restore thou them that are penitent; According to thy promises declared unto mankind in Christ Jesu our Lord. And grant, O most merciful Father, for his sake; That we may hereafter live a godly, righteous and sober life. To the Glory of thy holy Name. Amen.

CONTENTS

INTRODUCTION:
HUMAN UNITY IN SIN

I

THE GENERAL CONFESSION FIRST APPEARED IN THE
Prayer Book of 1552, and has remained unaltered from
that date. It is said at evening and morning prayer by
the whole congregation. That is not only to make sure
that everyone says it, whether (as in the past) he could
read it or not, but to emphasise its general character. It
is not an individual confession but the confession of the
Church: we participate in a general public act. This aspect of the confession is most important. We do not lose
our individuality when we say it, but we approach God
in and with the congregation. We declare publicly that
not only our own will, for which we are responsible, but
the general will, in which we share, is sinful. We share
in a social confession to which we give positive assent.

The very title, *General* Confession, shows that it is
not a private or sectional confession of particular persons or of groups and classes. It is spoken in the name of
those who go to Church and of those who never darken
her doors. It applies to the adulterer, the thief, the
swindler, the criminal of every sort, and equally to the
philanthropist, the just, the merciful and to the most
devout and exalted saint. It is true of the plumber, the

17

lawyer, the stockbroker, the statesman, the housewife, soldier and bishop. It is true of the Queen and the poorest of her subjects. It expresses the spiritual state of the Communist and the Conservative, the Modernist and the orthodox, even the neo-orthodox, the Protestant and the Catholic. It is especially true of every Englishman, Scot, Welsh, French, German, American and man of every land. The General Confession is the place where extremes meet; the most miserable sinner rubs shoulders with the Pope. Here all human distinctions and relativities are reduced to their real proportions. Here all men are brought into the presence of a Transcendent, Judging God, and all stand equally in need of His final mercy.

It is a confession, an admission of unworthiness, which is the necessary human approach to God; for unless we are conscious of our sinful state we are unable to receive God's grace. That consciousness itself is the gift of grace; but the acceptance of it, even the blind acceptance, is necessary to enable us to become aware of our relation to God. The natural man is not conscious of God, he is in darkness, however great his learning or however important his position; he can escape from that natural darkness and enter into the light of God only by humbling himself, recognising his unworthiness. This, then, is the first step, to make known our unworthiness, to open up, to put ourselves on the same level as everyone else, to give up our self-satisfaction and self-justification, to join in this corporate act of acknowledgment of sin.

II

The supreme irony of the human situation in every age is that the one and only thing in which all men are at one is sin. And the paradox is that sin makes any other unity imperfect if not impossible. The unity for which men strive in various ways is always negated by the unity for which they never need to strive— their unity in sin. This is the outstanding contradiction of human nature, which manifests itself in history and personal psychology. Because man is united with his fellow man in sin, he is forever divided from him. And because he himself is sinful from head to foot, in body and soul, he is a divided personality.

It is difficult for our generation to understand the thrill which that great battle-cry "Workers of the world unite; you have nothing to lose but your chains," [1] aroused the Europe of a hundred years ago. We who have seen the workers of the world twice in a single generation torn asunder in mutual extermination, and have witnessed the workers of a victorious revolution become an instrument for the oppression of the workers of a defeated revolution, have become hopelessly incapacitated from entering into the mind and heart of the millions who felt a new surge of hope when they first heard that cry. It became the symbol of emancipation, the first rosy dawn of a new liberty, and to the dream of working-class unity nameless thousands sacrificed their time, energy, prospects and substance.

[1] *Communist Manifesto* (1848).

We can trace the process in which this rainbow dream turned into the nightmare of today in the development of the various Internationals. The First International was founded by Marx, who assumed that the root of disunity was an external complex of class-relations. All history, said Marx, has been the history of class-struggle. Capitalism has so developed the age-long class-struggle, said he, that it has reduced the classes participating in the struggle to two—the proletariat and the bourgeoisie. Let the workers transcend their secondary divisions—for example, the national—and they will usher in the new classless society. Abolish the capitalist class—and society will enter upon the era in which it will become finally one.

III

Marx and Engels failed to secure even a semblance of unity. The First International which was composed of the leaders of the various national labour movements, not the rank-and-file, was riven by jealousies and rivalries. There was the conflict between Lassalle and Marx, which was resolved by the death of Lassalle in a duel; the bitter and vicious division between Marx and Bakunin, the famous old Russian anarchist, which destroyed the First International, for by removing its headquarters to New York, Marx defeated Bakunin at the cost of killing the International.[1] The hot gospeller

[1] E. H. Carr's *Life of Bakunin*.

of working-class unity discovered that his differences with other working-class leaders were irreconcilable. The International could not harbour two Popes at the same time. Either Marx or Bakunin. History settled the question by abolishing the International.

Of course, neither Marx nor Bakunin admitted for a moment that their conflict was one of personal power or domination. Marx could see it in Bakunin, and Bakunin could see it in Marx, neither could see it in himself. Each protagonist was convinced that he was defending the integrity of a policy or a principle. Whilst the policy or principle was real enough, it was at the same time the embodiment of a personal will-to-power. The basic self-righteous egotism of the leaders shattered the movement. That is to say, the sinfulness in which both Marx and Bakunin were at one made impossible their co-operation for ends which both regarded as supreme.

So the Second International, founded in 1900, was shattered by the First World War in 1914. When the Kaiser shook hands with the leaders of the German Social Democracy in August, 1914, and said that they were all Germans, that handshake squeezed Marxism to death; for it showed nationalism to be a stronger force than class. Neither Marx himself nor his greatest disciple, Lenin, ever made a grosser mistake than the underestimation of the power of nationalism. To the European worker, nation has always meant more than class. It meant more in 1914. It has come to mean more to the Russian of today than world-revolution. The sin in men which leads them to the elevation of nationality above humanity effectively prohibits class unity.

The Third International, founded by Lenin after the War, was the most powerfully disrupting force of all in the International Labour Movement. It divided the movement in Germany, and so smoothed the road to power for Hitler. It opposed working-class unity in Spain even in the midst of civil war. All this is fact, and not theory. The theory, of course, never recognises the sin of assertive egoism. It never admits that a quarrel about policy conceals a lust for power. It never allows for the inescapable disunity of sin.

Today we know that Communism, the primary aim of which is human unity, is the greatest cause of conflict the world has ever known. Wherever it spreads it threatens the integration of society. Its avowed technique is to create dissatisfaction and disruption, and to undermine order. Where it succeeds it is maintained by force, and the unity of which it boasts is held together by secret police and arms and the denial of freedom. For sin, in which men are one, splits them apart, only false unity is possible, there is no basis for reconciliation in their hearts and souls.

This lust for power is true even of our United Nations. The principles of the Charter are admirable, but the absolute sovereignty each nation claims makes the effective unity of the world impossible. The strains of different national policies and ambitions are not brought into harmony by the recognition of human well-being, so that the claims of national egotism, pride and self-interest, remain in irreconcilable conflict.

IV

We see the same signs of disunity in religion.

By a convention of the historian, we have come to think of the Mediaeval Church as a unity. But it was a unity only in contrast with the Church in modern Europe. It was a casual rather than an organic unity. It was not even that, if we remind ourselves of the great split between the East and the West, and, later, of the Great Schism, when rival Popes hurled anathemas at each other. The secessions of the Reformation, in spite of the appalling complex of corruption and disruption, would never have taken place if Popes and reformers had not been driven by personal will-to-power. But the fact is that whilst they were genuinely concerned with decisive issues they unconsciously insinuate into these very issues—Justification by Faith, Authority, The Word of God, Christian Liberty, etc. —their own sinful striving and lust of power, with the result that even the casual unity perished. The door was opened to the unfettered creation of schisms—a veritable cancer in the Body of Christ.

We can see the operation of the same spirit in the conflict between the Church of England and Puritanism. Will-to-power always tends to transform secondary differences into first-class issues, into questions of life and death. This is proved by the fact that the

23

seceder nearly always repeats the thing against which he protests. "New presbyter is old priest writ large", and generally without the acquired polish of the old priest. A hundred causes operated further to divide the Church of England. Seeping into them all was the unrealised trickle of poisonous self-righteousness and self-deception. And only God can decide whether the Anglican or the Puritan was the greater sinner.

The great cause of Church Reunion today would become practical politics if Christian men and women were to develop awareness that their championship of principles is not 100 per cent disinterested. This does not mean that the issues which divide us would lose their significance. I hope the day will never dawn when the Churches will reunite merely because they have grown tired of their divisions. That will mean a de-vitalised Church. But to the extent that we become aware of how we make great issues vehicles of our sinfulness, so shall we see the things that divide us in a new setting. In that process, a good deal of chaff will be separated from the wheat. Church unity does not mean that we should all be the same, act the same, and say the same words. It means rather that, given certain fundamentals (which are surprisingly few), our differences should become elements in an organic tension, like the string which makes a length of stick into a bow. So the Church would become the place where contradictions were maintained—not suppressed. Unity is not got by dissipating tensions and denying opposites: that leads to uniformity, which is a very different thing.

Both in secular and religious spheres, therefore, it is apparent how sin, egoistic assertion, self-centredness, makes real organic unity unrealisable. It used to be the jibe of the world against the Church that she could not unite. In these apocalyptic times, the world has demonstrated an even greater inability to act unitedly on almost any issue. United in sin, it remains divided in everything else.

v

The reason for this lies in the great theological fact that man has been created by God in His own image. That is to say man has been made to be the expression of the same will, to be the recipient and the channel of the same love, as in God.

Man is unique in his power of self-determination, in his capacity to will his own destiny. Every other form of organic life is created simply to take a path of development marked out for it from which it cannot depart. But, different from all other creatures, man is endowed with the mysterious, non-rational or super-rational power to will his own acts, with the immensely significant consequence that his line of development depends on the exercise of his power of choice. Man does not directly determine his biological growth, but he does determine what his mental, emotional and moral development will be. He has the power of self-assertion. He wills his acts. But because he is not alone, he becomes by his acts involved with the innumerable assertions of will of other individuals. This is the necessary condition of his existence.

Because of the power of self-determination man becomes a creator. Marx sensed this great theological truth in his economic theory of labour. Labour power, said Marx, was the only factor in production that was able to create new values, which is the economic way of saying that freedom is man's greatest possession, that man, out of his will, creates new possibilities. He literally makes history. History, in its totality, does not make man.

None of the critics of Marxism, so far as I know, has pointed out the profound contradiction between Marx's Labour-Theory of Value and his philosophy of man, that the individual is merely the ensemble of social relations. If the individual is merely a product, how can he create new values of any sort? History is the development of all the possibilities initiated by man.

Man is God's image primarily by virtue of his power of self-determination. It is in his freedom to will that man is like God. Our conception of creation has been too much influenced by the Platonic stress on imagination to the exclusion of the Biblical emphasis on will. In the Bible, it is the *will* of God that supremely matters. Will is the directing element in the dynamics of love. The ultimate significance of creation, therefore, is not rational or imaginative, but moral.

God created mankind as a unity in Himself, but with this awful power of self-determination. But at the core of this ability to be free there lies a paradox, as indeed there is in all Christian doctrine. Christ is God and Man. So man's freedom can function only as it is in subjection to God's will. Men can be free only if they are bound. They find fulfilment by subordinating their individual wills to God. When every individual finds his centre in the will of God, all wills become directed towards the same end; though the variety of wills is infinite, there is unity in difference. That is the one and only way in which mankind can be united—by being related to the same centre, by the acceptance of the same end.

Now in history we have to face the fact, however we may account for it, that the human race, through the individuals composing it, *has willed itself out of conscious relation with God*. That is the meaning of the Fall of Man: by disobedience man made himself his own centre. Without God as centre every individual becomes his own centre. This egocentricity necessarily tends towards the negation of every other egocentricity.

We are all desperately bent on being dictators, big or little. Being self-centred we are at the mercy of our mutual wills-to-power, our determination to be egocentric in the home, in our work, in politics, in Church, wherever we are. If we do not openly show it we keep it secretly in our hearts: outwardly subservient, inwardly lusting for power. This is the source of the contradiction in human nature which makes our good intentions go wrong; which ordains that our aspirations, in the process of their achievement, become self-defeating; which makes history a jig-saw puzzle of

27

50715

alternating bloom and decay; which sets every man's hand against his neighbour; which compels us to devote reason and science and culture to the service of death and stupidity, as even the blindest is aware in this nuclear age. Can anything be more idiotic than for civilised communities to deprive themselves of food and to utilise the materials and energies saved in this way to provide means of destruction for each other? Yet every nation feels it must do it! Behind this necessity lies man's refusal to be freely subject to God, his insistence on being his own God, on doing his own will. Since we are all alike in this, we are irrevocably divided from each other. United in sin, we become disunited in everything else. This is the shocking mess in which humanity finds itself, especially that part which regards itself as the progressive, civilised humanity of today.

VI

Thus the General Confession is profoundly relevant to our human situation and to the tragic state of the world. There are all sorts of arguments against the General Confession. We can argue, for instance, that Church people don't take it seriously. They will repeat in Church that they "are miserable sinners", but would be gravely offended if somebody accused them of being such in private. And that is true. We all react badly to any hint that we are unworthy. We may argue that the Confession is out of date. Or we may challenge its truth. But can we justifiably assert that it is remote from our real world of frustration and failure, irrelevant to our personal lives as we have to live them today? There is nothing in the Prayer Book so sharply, acidly applicable to the world in its present state of confusion and uncertainty, and to individual men and women in their perplexity as the General Confession. Concentrated within it is contemporary history and personal psychology.

We repeat in words the General Confession on Sundays, and whether we are conscious of it or not, we live it in actual deed and being on week-days. Not a day goes by that we do not demonstrate, by the irrefutable argument of fact, "that there is no health in us". In the studies of the psycho-analysts there is a mounting accumulation of commentary on the General Confession. It illumines the whole tragedy of human life. Nothing can be more pertinent, then, than the endeavour to penetrate the meaning of this cry of sinful man, a cry from the deep abyss of his soul.

One

GOD AS HOLY, OMNIPOTENT LOVE

"Almighty and Most Merciful Father . . ."

I

THE WORDS OF THE INVOCATION EXPRESS THE manner in which we make our approach to God. He is almighty. Almighty, the very first word, gives us pause. Almighty means power, all power, limitless, the primacy, the Absolute; and to the Almighty we bow down and confess. In His presence we declare our certain nothingness. To the lofty one, high above all, beyond nature, beyond principalities and powers, to the centre of gravity of existence, we address ourselves. Let us take account of what we say, and the words we use. As we say "Almighty God" we are at one of the most tremendous moments of our lives, not less tremendous because the words are in our prayers morning and evening. Do not let us ever say them casually or merely formally or while only half awake. To say them is to affirm God and that the entire world of man is dependent upon Him.

To be almighty means that He answers to none but Himself. All other powers, whatever they be, in

31

Church or State, and in society at large, in every institution, as well as in individual men, are limited, subject to law, capable of being challenged. Only absolute power is unlimited, the almighty power of God.

Yet as we know, there are powers among men that claim to be absolute. Lord Acton epitomised the human law of power when he wrote, "Power tends to corrupt; absolute power corrupts absolutely." How can we justify the absolute power of God? Is God a tyrant? The answers to these questions, which have troubled men from the beginning, are that God is absolute as the Creator, and His power is Love. Absolute power which is wholly in God is incorruptible because of love, because God gives Himself utterly, His interests being ours. He gives Himself, not merely good things, not mere promises, but His actual self, in the Incarnation. There is nothing that God withholds from us—all is yours, says the Apostle, things present and things to come, all yours: there could be no greater generosity of love and no more complete justification of omnipotence.

II

Power is an essential element in human life. Without it nothing could exist and life would perish. It is power that keeps families intact, power that enables institutions to survive, power that makes society possible. But political theory—which is the theory of relations between people and societies of people—from Plato to de Jouvenel, recognises that human power cannot be trusted. "Power tends to corrupt." Democracy is a clear recognition of the inevitable degeneration of power, since it sees the essence of politics in checking power. A brief consideration of some phases of social development establishes this fact beyond possibility of doubt.

Despite the great horrors that face our society, we look back with amazement on the first half of the nineteenth century when the evils and abuses of the Industrial Revolution were at their height. How was it possible for a professedly Christian community to tolerate the terrible wrongs suffered by the working-classes up to the inauguration of what is rather ineptly called the Welfare State? The callousness of early Victorian England seems to us almost incredible. Some of the best men in that society saw in the dreadful poverty of the time a divine dispensation.[1] Let us note one or two examples.

The cruelty with which children were treated in mines, domestic service and "the dark satanic mills" was beyond belief. They were made to work long hours in the most insanitary conditions. In the best factories, the average working day *for children* was fourteen hours, which was often exceeded, for when the factories were especially busy, children used to work from 3 a.m. to 10.30 p.m. And in the course of their work in certain spinning processes, where they

[1] See *The Town Labourer*, by J. L. and Barbara Hammond, Chapters X and XI.

had to follow moving machinery, it was estimated that children walked about thirty-five miles a day, and would get so exhausted that they could only be driven to their work by the strap. Here is an excerpt from the evidence of a mill overlooker. "These children every moment they have to spare, will be stretched all their length upon the floor in a state of perspiration, and we are obliged to keep them up to the work by using either a strap or some harsh language, and they are kept continually in a state of grief, though some of them cannot shed tears . . . They are always in terror . . ." And here is the evidence of a child who worked from 5 a.m. to 8 p.m. "Yes, I was strapped most severely, till I could not bear to sit upon a chair without having pillows, and I was forced to lie upon my face in the night time at one time, and through that I left; I was strapped both on my own legs and then I was put upon a man's back and then strapped, and buckled with two straps to an iron pillar and flogged . . ."

Workhouses and orphanages hired out the children to the mills. After the Napoleonic wars there were left thousands of orphans, whom the ratepayers did not want to support, who were herded like cattle to the mills and mines. Some parishes insisted that with every twenty mentally sound children taken there should be one idiot.

Cruelty to children was only one aspect of the horrors of the Industrial Revolution. Women were worked like beasts of burden from fourteen to sixteen hours a day in coal-mines. Employers were guided by two principles—to get the maximum work out of their employees for the minimum cost.

How could such iniquities be perpetrated? For the men committing these cruelties were, in their ordinary relations, kindly and decent and of average virtue. They were mostly Liberal and Nonconformist, and neither Liberalism nor Nonconformity put a premium upon cruelty. Conservatives and Anglicans acted in exactly the same way. It was not the mere result of the factory system; for children were similarly abused in domestic and craft services.

The root reason for this appalling brutality lay in the fact of power—that one human being was in the power of another. The manufacturers of early Victorian England proved that they could not be trusted with economic power. Parliament was compelled to impose severe restrictions on their use of power with regard to hours and conditions of labour. The greater the power exercised over human beings, the greater the cruelty to which it degenerates.

In America conditions were the same, and in addition there were the horrors of slavery. There as everywhere were high-minded protests, but slavery continued for many years. Within our own lifetime in Britain we know how extensive was the misery of unemployment and how millions suffered throughout the world because of the misuse of economic power.

We see the same corruption of power in personal and family relationships. Our statute books bear witness to the fact that the largest and most powerless minority in the world—children—have had to be protected against their parents. But parental cruelties which the law restricts are of the more obvious, coarse and simple kind. The power-striving of parent against child, of husband against wife, and vice versa, is something with which law cannot deal. There is a whole range of subtle cruelty and tyranny which camouflages itself in the guise of altruism and love. It is in the name of love that a wife will stifle her husband's personality and freedom, and in the same way a husband will crush every seed of spiritual life in his wife. Power is hydra-headed: crush it here and it will assume a new form there.

In our world of advanced technology and the development of nuclear power with its incredible possibilities this problem of power has entered upon a new and more sinister phase, in which the issue at stake is nothing less than the continued possibility of man's existence on the earth. Increasing power over nature has increased man's destructive use of power over his fellows. An ever-increasing proportion of the energies and wealth of the nations is being devoted to preparations for warfare, and statesmen appear to be incapable of mastering the situation that confronts them. Power is escaping out of their hands. The most innocent economic and domestic uses of nuclear power have war potential as their basis and what could bring inestimable blessing to mankind may be its greatest curse because of the moral failure of those who have the ruling power in society. Today, the will-to-power feeds and grows on the increased capacity of power to suppress and destroy. In Bertrand Russell's words: "There is no hope for the world unless power can be tamed and brought into the service, not of this or that group of fanatical tyrants, but of the whole human race, white and yellow and black, fascist and communist and democrat; for science has made it inevitable that all must live or all must die."

Cinema, radio, television as well as the press are means of power that can be used to control the minds and souls of people. In the name of art and freedom these powers may be used to pervert and enslave millions, even without the victims knowing it. The techniques of publicity and propaganda are constantly perfected so that the interests of those who hold power can be protected and extended. Modern power can compel men to think according to the will of tyrants. Subtle forms of dictatorship thus become dominating inside the citadel of the soul.

Together with the growth of power there has proceeded increased ruthlessness and demoralisation. Everywhere and in every sphere power tends to corrupt, and the nearer man approaches to the possession of absolute power, the more satanic and cruel he becomes. This growth of power bids fair to wreck human existence.

In human hands absolute power corrupts absolutely. There is no challenging that assertion: neither king nor priest, neither dictator nor president, neither race nor nation, neither party nor group is exempt. Therefore, absolute allegiance cannot be owed to anything human. We dare not swear unconditional obedience to the State or to the Church, for such absolute obedience will inevitably tend to be used in the service of evil.

III

In truth, absolute power, the greatest evil of international politics, does not exist. It is an illusion; for when it comes to the test it is challenged by war. It is a false claim that must be given up. Only God has power that cannot be challenged. Here the General Confession affirms of God what is unknown in the whole realm of human experience. It begins with a most daring paradox; that in God absolute power is united with absolute mercy. "Almighty and most merciful Father" asserts not merely that God is love, but that God is almighty love. In man, power is used to suppress and destroy. In God, power is redemptive and constructive. It is not enough to say that God is love. What is the use of powerless love? Of what value is a love that cannot cope with the world's sin and tragedy? What is the Cross without the Resurrection? "If Christ be not raised from the dead," if Love is not also omnipotent, "we are of all men the most miserable."

God as almighty raises one of the most difficult of all theological problems—the problem of omnipotence. Is God Almighty? True to the genius of the Christian perception of God, the General Confession leaves us in no doubt about the answer to this question. It begins with an affirmation of the divine omnipotence.

The late Dr. Forsyth—one of the outstanding European theologians of the twentieth century—said that most of the so-called *problems* in theology were due to the fact that they represented secular ideas which had not undergone the process of baptism into Christ. That is, they were ideas originating from a human viewpoint and incorporated into Christian theology without being reshaped in terms of Christian experience. This is peculiarly true of the idea of omnipotence. It has chiefly been thought of as *power to impose will, as power to remove resistance by force*. Has God the power to impose His will upon unwilling objects? Put in that way, the question violates the very essence of the New Testament revelation of God. It is a subtle, almost unconscious, expression of human pride masquerading in the guise of theology. As though one were to say: "I am prepared to believe in this God of yours and in His power if He will do what I think He should do."

Throughout human history and experience, the test of the reality of power has been the ability to impose one's own will. That, for example, has been the supreme quest in political conflict. Society accepted the power of a king when he gave evidence of his ability to crush opponents, and the same with governments. Communism equates power with ability to remove opposition, without any attempt at camouflaging its action, and Marxist theories of the state formulate the final logic of power politics, for they reduce the state to the ultimate, fundamental element of force glorified by the phrase "the dictatorship of the proletariat". But all political systems now existing in the world ultimately regard power in the same terms. It is ability to enforce its own will, whatever may be the differences (which may be great) in the uses to which power is put. It is to this that political theory, in its development from the Greek City-State through the mediaeval universal state to the modern nation-state, even in its democratic forms, has come. Power is thought to be the ability to make opposition ineffective or to destroy it.

The same is true, though in a more involved way, in social life. In modern industrial life, power means the right of the nationalised or private enterprise corporation to have its own way, the ability to impose its will. Trade-unionism is the history of the effort to limit the power of the employer: it has become a means of exerting power by workmen over workmen, and by unions over the public at large, holding the public to ransom for higher wages, for instance.

Even in the institution which comes nearest to personality, the family, power has been envisaged as ability to be supreme against all opposition. In ancient Rome the father was very nearly absolute. His rights over wife and children were unchallenged. In Western civilisation there has been a progressive delimitation of the powers of the head of the family. It has taken centuries of struggle to achieve personal status for women and children within the family. Freudian psychology bears witness to the ancient omnipotence of the father, and to its devastating effects in the life of the individual. In the final analysis, omnipotence is conceived in terms of power against power, of will opposed to will. The test of omnipotence is precisely the ability to crush opposition. Force is the ultimate method by which omnipotence can make its will effective.

Now the basic error in most of the thinking about omnipotence is that it starts from this false premise of pride. Certainly if omnipotence means power to make will effective by the forcible overcoming of opposition, it is quite clear that God does not deal with opposition in that way, whether He can do so or not. The existence of evil is the incontestable proof that God is not a dictator. Thus evil becomes the source of the most stubborn problem of the secular mind. Evil becomes an insoluble problem when man insists that God must be the same as himself. If we assume that power means the same thing to God as it does to sinful man, then we are faced with the celebrated dilemma of modern secularism: either God is omnipotent and not good, because He allows evil, or, if He is good, then He is not omnipotent—which is the familiar short cut to atheism. A powerless God is no God at all. This was the root of Ivan Karamazov's atheism in Dostoievsky's novel *The Brothers Karamazov*. In his mind, the final condemnation of God was the suffering of the children. "It's not worth the tears of that one tortured child who beat itself on the breast with its little fist and prayed in its stinking outhouse, with its unexpiated tears to 'dear, kind God'! It's not worth it, because those tears are unatoned for . . . And if the sufferings of children go to swell the sum of sufferings which was necessary to pay for truth, then I protest that the truth is not worth such a price." How often has it been said—for example, by James Thomson in his *City of Dreadful Night* —that a God who looks upon the dreadful suffering of humanity without preventing it, when He has the power to do so, is a devil. This is the final conclusion of pride, the satanic challenge to God to become like unto man.

Omnipotence, thus formulated, violates the essence of the New Testament revelation of God as love. Correctly understood, omnipotence is love in action. Together, omnipotence and love constitute the unity of God's being. They can be understood only in relation to each other. Separated they become meaningless: love degenerates into sentimentalism and omnipotence into force and immorality. No wonder then that omnipotence in the terms of human thinking becomes an insoluble problem.

IV

"God is Love" is the great revealing word of the Bible about God, and all Christian thinking about God starts from this point, which involves a radical departure from all secular philosophies. God, in the whole of His relationship to men, is love. The Bible, in

42

conceivable: omnipotence can not only bring forth the most imposing of all things, the world in its visible totality, but it can create the most delicate of all things, a creature independent of it. Omnipotence which can lay its hand so heavily upon the world can also make its touch so light that the creature receives independence. It is only a miserable and worldly picture of the dialectic of power to say that it becomes greater in proportion as it can compel and make things dependent. Socrates knew better; the art of using power is to make free. But between men that can never happen, though it may always be necessary to stress that it is the greatest good: only omnipotence can do so in truth." [1]

Hence, to say that God is love is the same thing as to say that God is almighty. "Almighty *and* most merciful Father." It is only omnipotence that can give freedom without desiring to exercise it either on behalf of or instead of the recipient. This is what Kierkegaard means when he says that omnipotence takes *itself* back —not the gift itself, not the freedom which it gives— in the act of giving. The Giver dissociates Himself from His gift, so that the recipient may exercise the gift he has received quite independently. Man's self-determination is real. Divine omnipotence is manifested in the reality of human freedom.

Three considerations make this view of omnipotence clear.

First, it surely does not need much argument to

[1] Theodore Haecker, *Søren Kierkegaard*, pp. 18–19 (Oxford University Press, 1937).

demonstrate that it is beyond human capacity for one human being or group to permit another being or group real independence in the use of freedom. Even with the best will in the world men and women, in the most subtle ways, conscious and unconscious, endeavour to trespass on one another's freedom. And with the worse or worst will, suppression of freedom becomes a primary end. In other words, will-to-power, either in the form of naked force and aggression, or in some rationalised guise of morality and culture, is an all-pervading principle in human relationships. We have already had some evidence of this in the preceding discussion, and we shall have occasion to consider still more evidence in a later chapter. Directly or indirectly, we are perpetually seeking to impose ourselves on others. The process begins in the cradle. Indeed according to Alfred Adler, the process begins in the womb. And it does not end even in the grave. Think of the terms of many human wills. We can see this lust for power, this effort to exercise the gift of freedom for and instead of others, throughout history which in sum is the tale of conflicting egoisms. The struggle for liberty by suppressed nations and classes degenerates into a struggle for the right and opportunity to become tyrannical in turn. This is the outstanding lesson in every revolution. We see will-to-power operating in social and industrial history. Half the quarrels inside the working-class movements are about power under high-sounding principles. We see it in the history of the Churches, especially in that of the Roman and the

Calvinist Genevan. Calvin and the Popes differed in nearly everything except in believing that the safety of Christianity was bound up with their personal supremacy. Modern psychology has taught us to see will-to-power in the most intimate relationships of men, women and children. The one thing we will not do, *cannot* do, is to regard the freedom of another as inviolable. In New Testament language, we cannot purely love our fellow-creatures. In theory and in the abstract, yes. But in actual hard fact, no. As Ivan Karamazov put it: "To my thinking, Christ-like love for men is a miracle impossible on earth. He was God. One can love one's neighbours in the abstract, or even at a distance, but at close quarters it's almost impossible." Count Mirabeau was known as the Friend of Man, and was very forward in good works for the peasantry, but he hated and tortured his son, the famous Mirabeau of the Revolution. One of the great tasks facing the Church today is to re-educate her own people, professing Christians, about what New Testament love means. The Church has to witness to itself and the world that what so many Christians think of as love is not at all identifiable with the New Testament reality. To love with purity, without egoism, is to be completely objective towards another's freedom.

In the second place, it is surely obvious that there has been no divine trespass upon man's freedom as witnessed in the often asked question, Why does God tolerate pain and horror in the world? In wartime, the problem is summed up in the question: Why does God allow war? And today, why does He allow the terror of the hydrogen bomb?

The suffering and pain of the world are evidence of God's will to respect personality, just as they are evidence of man's failure to respect it. This is what the secular mind cannot understand. And the paradox is that it is the best men—not the worst—who are most sensitive to the world's pain and tragedy. Had they the power, they would prevent it. But how? There are only two ways by which suffering can be prevented. First, by depriving man of self-will, in which case all experience—pleasure as well as pain—loses moral meaning. For cows there is no *problem* of suffering. It may exist for them as a fact, but never as a problem. And, second, suffering can be abolished by complete recognition of mutual freedom. There's no other way. And both are beyond human power. History is the record of the unceasing effort to deprive men of freedom. The boldest bid to end freedom has been made in our day by the totalitarian systems. And during the war and today humanity pays indirect tribute to God's love, to His ineffable goodness, in its recognition that suffering is preferable to tyranny.

When it is accepted, suffering loses its contradiction. In these circumstances, it is not-suffering that becomes a problem. In a unique situation, when tragedy and tyranny become alternative issues for the world, suffering is embraced almost as a joy. When the maximum of pain is inflicted on humanity, it is precisely at that point that it approximates to a minimum as a problem.

When freedom is regarded as the supreme good, suffering becomes incidental—dreadful, cruel, colossal—yet incidental. If political freedom, civic freedom, social freedom can be so priceless to sinful man, what can personal freedom, which involves and transcends all other freedoms, mean to a perfect, loving God?

And this brings us to our third consideration.

The personal freedom—the redemption—of every man, woman and child means, to God, the Cross. It is so overwhelming a desire in the heart of God that, in Christ, He shrank not from the supreme suffering of death. The Cross is the historic symbol of God's omnipotence, of His infinite capacity to endure any and every evil that man can perpetuate so that, through the endurance of it, men will achieve their freedom. The Cross is the assurance that nothing turns God aside from His will, that human freedom achieves its final reality.

In actual human experience, men and women feel and endure only their own individual suffering, and, at most, that of their immediate family and friends. It is very rare that people feel, as their own, any pain and suffering beyond their immediate circle. To tolerate the sufferings of other people is easy so long as these same sufferings do not assail our own hearts and minds. We can even make eloquent speeches about them and sign petitions of protest. All this means very little. It is the rarest thing for men and women to realise in themselves, as a personal experience, the pain of people beyond their ken. Only saints achieve such a height. And they are very few, a handful, one supposes, of religious recluses who have made a vocation of feeling the world's pain. And, mostly, the emotion such saints inspire in sane practical people, and in the fussy raucous progressives and reformers and revolutionaries, is anything from anger to contempt. They spend their days and a great part of the nights in feeling in their hearts the world's sin and pain—and praying for the world. But they are very, very few. What does the *world's* suffering mean to the vast majority of us, even when we become aware of it? What difference to our way of living have the horrors suffered by people during the last twenty years made to us in terms of *personal* sacrifice?

But what is merely an abstraction to us, in God becomes a living reality. God feels the pain and disaster of every human being as His own; for in Him all mankind are one. Any attempt to describe how God feels the pain and sin of the world would strain language into the most fantastic imageries. Indeed, God feels the suffering of an individual man or woman more acutely and significantly than he or she ever can feel it. God endures every pain, every horror, every tragedy, every sin—and in spite of all, does not crush freedom. He suffers and pursues His divine conspiracy for the redemption of the thing He made a soul. How can He bear it? That is the mystery of His omnipotence, the miracle also of His love. "Almighty and most merciful Father." Thus omnipotence is not a capacity for performing metaphysical acrobatics. It is the totality of God's relation to man and the world. It is His being.

V

"Most merciful," we say, for we approach a merciful God. "Blessed are the merciful," said Jesus, "for they shall obtain mercy." Without mercy our lives would be fruitless, and without the revelation that mercy is God's nature, we should not dare to approach Him. For every one of us needs mercy, which is the specific activity of God towards the helpless. We need mercy and can expect it. That is what makes possible our confession. Because in His mercy God lets us know that He will receive us mercifully we can approach Him with confidence.

We ask for mercy later on in the confession but at the moment we think of the Almighty Father as the merciful one. His eye upon us is not indifferent. He does not accept us strangely. He looks upon us, each of us individually, the congregation of which we are a part, and the human race to which we belong, with mercy. So we have no fear.

Furthermore, we say "Father". God has revealed Himself as Father through the Son, and as our Father we owe Him obedience. The revelation of our relation to God is that of sons. This assertion of God's nature and ours should be clearly in our mind. When we say "Father" we have come home; we are in His house, wherever we are. In Church we say "Father" in the congregation,—good and bad, white and black, rich and poor, all sons and daughters of God, all welcome at His mercy seat.

This is a tremendous assertion that we are making, that the ineffable God, creator of all things, the infinite One whose rule is throughout infinite space, the unseen, the unknowable, the Eternal, is our merciful Father. We approach Him with awe that fills all the recesses of heart and mind. We kneel before Him. And we say "Merciful Father", recognising our obligation to Him. We all come to the Eternal Being and say the same words, acknowledging our obligation to Him. We owe ourselves to Him. And in humility and trust we make our confession.

Two

THE ORIGINAL SIN
OF REBELLION

"We have erred and strayed from Thy ways like lost sheep. We have followed too much the devices and desires of our own hearts. We have offended against Thy Holy Laws."

I

AT ONCE WE DECLARE OUR FAULT; WE HAVE ERRED and strayed. The earth is, in Karl Barth's words, "our theatre of revolt", and we admit it. We admit our rebellion. We admit our mistakes, our manifold mistakes: even when we strive to do well, we erred. A very hard thing to do, to own up to being wrong, as we are so often! We err with our families, our neighbours, with those with whom we work, this we must admit as we look into our hearts. Above all, we have erred and strayed from Thy ways, O loving God. Thy ways are the ways of eternity, and we have chosen the ways of the world . . . like lost sheep, like silly sheep, following the devices and desires of our own hearts, which belong to the world.

In the invocation we affirm that God is almighty and loving. He is also holy. "We have offended against Thy holy laws." Just as omnipotence and love become intelligible only in relation to the experience of man in history, so, too, holiness acquires meaning and significance in the same process. To treat the divine being and character as mere abstraction is to deprive God of reality. In history as a realm of freedom the omnipotence, love and holiness of God become real and relevant.

So it is not enough to say that God is love. Because of the secularisation and degeneration of the modern world, that simple and profound assertion is liable to grave misunderstanding. Our world has almost lost the capacity to understand what love, in the Biblical sense, means. God's love is not the sentimental feeling that goes by the name of love in our human intercourse. It is holy. In God's love there is an ultimate centre and core of rock; an ultimate which is continuously operative in historical development and personal experience. "We have offended against Thy holy laws" is the General Confession manner of saying that the God we are dealing with is a Sovereign who cannot be challenged. God is holy and irresistible. We have offended against the holiness of God. With humble awareness we realise that we have violated His holiness. We know it. In history and experience man is also aware of it, but obstinately refuses to admit the fact. Proof? *Man's universal and inescapable sense of guilt.*

Reduced to its essence, what does guilt mean? It is of the first importance to understand that it is something personal. It is not abstract or merely institutional. It is personal. When I feel that I have done something which I *ought* not to have done, I am affirming two fundamental facts, at least. First, that I was invading and violating the rights of another; and, second, that I need not have done so. The blame is not something I can pass on. It is mine. Guilt is a component of trespass and responsibility. I have taken to myself something to which I have no right, something which was the inviolable, inalienable being of another. Guilt is the realisation of offence against an ultimate sanctity; that I have taken to myself what in the nature of things does not belong to me. In other words something sacred.

Now, one of the profoundest facts in the entire realm of history is that this sense of guilt is universal. It is part and parcel of the peculiar make-up of the human being. One is not human without it. It is the root of the radical disintegration of personality. Wherever we turn in history or experience, we are always faced by this fact of guilt. It was one of the most characteristic features of primitive man. The evidence from anthropology is practically unanimous. Taboo was the predominant institution of primitive society. And the argument which attempts to minimise the significance of primitive taboo by dwelling on its superstitious content is merely silly, and misses the point entirely. The overwhelmingly significantly thing is that primitive man was obsessed by fear of taboo, the ancient form of guilt. The most widely diverse societies were at one in this, at least, that they were ridden by a sense of guilt. It must have been very deep rooted to have survived the disproving by progressing experience of the particular details of the taboo itself. When, for example, it transpired that contact with corpses did not result in immediate death, the sense of guilt was not thereby dissipated. It simply found a new social embodiment.

In the history of civilisation, guilt has been equally predominant and all-pervading. Note, for example, how universal has been the institution of sacrifice in all ancient religions; whatever the difference is between them they were united in their recognition that man offends his gods and that their anger must be placated. How incredibly shallow is the rationalist attitude to this fact! The fear of the Gods, if you please, was the invention of priests! Deep down in the roots of his being, ancient man knew that he had "offended against Thy holy laws".

II

Guilt is the permanent theme, in different forms, of the world's great literature. Take Greek drama in its greatest period. Its grand problem was guilt. How the problem was solved was not a matter of primary importance. What is significant is the degree to which the Greek mind was obsessed by the problem, and as they came to maturity, the Greeks became more intensely aware of the all-pervading fact of guilt.

What is true of Greek drama is true also of all great European literature. Take two such examples as

Dostoievsky and Conrad. In *Crime and Punishment* and *Lord Jim* there are two characters, Raskolnikoff and Lord Jim, who symbolise the universality of the feeling of guilt in every human being. The significance of their respective crimes was not merely the wrong committed against any particular human beings, but that in the depth of their being they were out of accord with the nature of things. That is, they were obsessed with the fact of guilt. Their concern was not an isolated event, but the light cast by the isolated event upon their inner being.

Wherever men are most human, there they are most conscious of the profound cleavage in their nature, and the better they become, the more they grow in goodness, the more acute becomes their consciousness of sin. Awareness of guilt in some form or other is universal.

Kierkegaard pointed out the confusion that arises from treating sin as belonging to the sphere of ethics where there is no place for the concept. Sin has to do with man's relation to God not to virtue, and only in that sense has it any meaning. Original sin is sinfulness, the state in which man is born, his natural state of estrangement from God, which no virtue can remove. His acquired sins are his continued estrangement, which must inevitably increase however ethical he may be, until that estrangement is ended.

Nothing is so sinister in our world today as the decline of the sense of sin, the dissipating of the sense of guilt. It is literally a process of de-humanisation, of producing a race of anti-humanity. In his macabre story, *The Island of Dr. Moreau*, H. G. Wells described the experiments of a scientist in an attempt to breed a new race of beings from the sexual congress of apes and men. As in much of his earlier imaginative work Wells, divined only too well "the shape of things to come". The weakening of the sense of guilt from the consciousness of man would more than fulfil Wells' vision of the experimentation of Dr. Moreau. Man without guilt would be neither man nor ape. He would be an inconceivable monstrosity.

To this tendency, a great deal of well-intentioned thinking has unwittingly contributed, even much theology. The Liberal Protestant apotheosis of man, with his natural progress of perfection, bears some responsibility. So does aggressive secularism, and ethical humanism and good paganism. It is like the action of thoughtless children who persist in chipping away bits of mortar between the bricks of a building. Nobody is more surprised than the culprits when the building collapses.

These tendencies reach their full term in Freud. By this I do not mean what is of indubitable scientific achievements in the work of the Freudian school—the discovery of the Id (unconscious), the psycho-therapeutic method, etc. I mean rather the philosophical materialist assumptions of Freudianism masquerading as psychological science, just as the assumptions of the mechanical materialists masqueraded as physical science. Freudianism is much more destructive, not only of Christianity, but of civilisation, democracy and political and civic liberty, than the bluff materialism of the Haeckels and Buchners of an earlier generation, and the amiable Julian Huxleys and Fred Hoyles of this. At the risk of being dubbed fantastic, I venture to say that the fact that Hitlerism and Freudianism both originated in Vienna is, at least, striking. Freud, who saw (quite rightly) that suppressed guilt-feeling was the source of neurosis, paved the way for Hitler, a man of absolute egocentricity, to whom no right was sacred. And the irony was that one of Hitler's monsters turned Freud, in his old age, out of Vienna. When the sense of guilt goes, everything goes. Nothing remains sacred.

III

One of the arguments against a sense of sin, especially when it is intense, is that it has a tendency to make its possessors morbid. And that is indeed true. Only angels can afford to go to extremes without peril or injury. Yet absence of sense of guilt-feeling is a still greater peril for man and the entire human adventure. The morbidity which may develop from a sense of sin is a jovial sanity compared to the morbidity which most certainly does develop from the absence of it. The sickness which sense of sin may produce is much better for civilisation than the diseased mentality engendered by lack of it. Calvinism, for example, was less a peril to Western civilisation than Nazism.

But the sense of guilt never in fact disappears though

its presence is not admitted. However successful our generation may be in suppressing its sense of guilt, in tucking it away out of sight, complete success is impossible. "Out of sight" does not mean "out of mind". Guilt remains in the deep recesses of the mind. Neurosis conveys it, or hysteria. Nothing—literally nothing—can allay "the eternal restlessness of mortal man". There is no thicket in which he can hide himself from storms of self-accusation, no shore that cannot be washed by the recurrent tides of brooding aware-ness. The jauntiest and cockiest of generations and individuals sense its Damoclean presence. Indeed and indeed, whatever may be ghostly in the being and character of God, it will not be His holiness. All history thunders it to the heavy ears of mankind.

IV

In what does the holiness of God consist? What is this ultimate in God which is forever inviolable? Here again we must seek the answer in the realm of freedom.

In the revelation of the Bible, God did not create man merely free, but free *and dependent upon himself.* In his original state, as he came from the hands of God, man was self-determining and exercised his power of self-determination in conscious, voluntary subjection to God. Of his own free will he chose God's will. He joyfully acknowledged God's sovereignty over him. Man's original state was freedom in relation to God's almightiness.

The Original Sin of Rebellion

Now the primal disaster of humanity, of which history is the consequence, is that man departed from this original relation of freedom in subjection to God and appropriated to himself the right to act for himself. He attempted to wrest from God what only God can exercise. That was humanity's fall into self-centredness —man's original sin. It was a declaration of cosmic civil war. By the affirmation of his own ego, man put himself in God's place. The holiness of God consists in the unity of His omnipotence and love. His holiness is His eternal NAY to man in his state of rebellion.

The universe is moral. That is, it is so fashioned that any and every effort of man to be self-sufficient, self-existent, self-dependent, is doomed to defeat. History is dominated by the dialectic of self-frustration. We shall see evidence of this fact when we come to consider the corruption of human nature. God's holiness manifests itself in the process of judgment, which is a continuous, never-ceasing process in human life and history.

This is the irrefragable reality which the General Confession recognises in the words "we have offended against Thy holy laws". History is the tragic tale of offences. In the confession man's sin against god is brought into the open light of day. Modern man has been doing exactly the opposite, with what dreadful consequences even the blindest can see: he has been suppressing his consciousness of guilt. As Freud quite rightly states, this suppressed guilt-feeling creates havoc in the individual psyche. Indeed it does!

Psycho–neurosis is the reverse side of God's holiness. The cure for this is not the psycho–analytic humbug of bringing the suppressed guilt-complex into consciousness so as to banish it. That is the latest form of man's fatal delusion of human omnipotence. The cure is that which is prescribed in the General Confession— the bringing of the suppressed guilt-feeling into consciousness, *and to keep it there, as the humble recognition that only God can be sovereign.* To banish guilt is the sure and certain road to damnation.

"Almighty and most merciful Father . . . we have offended against Thy holy laws." God is love! He is Omnipotent, all-merciful and HOLY! Trinity in unity and unity in trinity.

v

No doctrine of the Church has been so derided and rejected as that of Original Sin. The modern world has come to look upon it as the greatest symbol of superstition and obscurantism in the whole range of Christian theology. No doctrine is so outrageous an offence to the contemporary estimate of human nature. It is so utterly incompatible with the rationalist delusion of the perfectibility of human nature that it is not so much argued out of existence as jeered away. It is now supposed to be relegated to the limbo of superseded superstitions. So completely has it been dismissed, that, even in contexts to which the doctrine seems to be peculiarly relevant, it strikes people as out of date and irrational. A personal incident will illustrate what I mean.

Surveying the ruins of a house in a badly-blitzed town in the west of England during the war, I remarked to the owner, a lady of really fine character, that here was original sin in operation. She turned to me with a look of pained surprise and said: "But surely, Mr. Davies, you don't believe in that dreadful doctrine?" To which I replied: "Such dreadful happenings as these"—pointing to the ruins—"demand some sort of dreadful doctrine in explanation." Here was a woman, one of the best representatives of our life and way of thinking, staring at death and devastation wrought by deliberate human will, who could see only something "dreadful" in the Christian affirmation of original sin. Nothing, in hard fact, could be more terrible than the destruction, mutilation and terror she had witnessed with her own eyes. Nothing could be more insulting to modern man's dream about human nature than the horrible bombing of defenceless children. Nevertheless, you must not utter the words original sin! So profound has become the aversion to the Christian challenge to human pride with its peacock's feathers.

That the doctrine of original sin can be a serious sociological hypothesis is inconceivable to minds shaped and moulded by scientific triumphs and social progress and deeply cultivated illusions about the nature of humanity. Yet how supremely relevant to man's situation in history is the doctrine of original sin and how realistic it is are entirely unfamiliar notions! There is profound incompatibility between the assumptions about the capacity of human nature which post-Renaissance Europe came to entertain and the Biblical doctrine of man a sinner in need of grace and redemption. What! This creature in need of redemption who is conquering space and time, who is fashioning utopia, who is abolishing disease, who is on the way to banishing poverty and other social evils, and conquering space with his artificial satellites? Nonsense!

Of course this attitude was made easier by the forms in which the doctrine of original sin was expressed. If you identify the doctrine with the exploits of two mythical ancestors in a legendary Garden of Eden, nothing is easier than to throw it overboard altogether, especially when at the same time, it conflicts with your feeling and estimate about your own worth. The deep irrationality of the unconscious mind co-operates with the superficial rationality of the conscious mind. Biology knows nothing of two ancestors, Adam and Eve. Anthropology knows nothing of a primitive Golden Age as a pre-historical fact.

But does it follow that if legends are proved to be devoid of literal, historical truth they have no truth of any kind? Have myths, then, no moral, spiritual or psychological significance? Even such materialists as Freud and his disciples refuse such a view. A whole school of psychological interpretation has grown up on the assumption that myths are of the profoundest significance for psychology and history. Note, for example, the work of Jung, the Swiss psychologist. But for all their blazing triumphs, psychologists cannot be permitted to monopolise mythology. The despised and rejected theologian, too, must be allowed to share.

So we must distinguish between shell and kernel, between accident and essence. The really important question about the story of the Garden of Eden is not, is it literally factually true, but, does it faithfully represent the truth about man's situation in history? Indeed, myths for this purpose can be much nearer the truth than documented history or rationally formulated statements.

What is myth? In essence, it is a representation of the facts and reality of existence without rationalisation. There is no attempt to iron out the contradictions of experience, which are preserved in their painful tension. That is why myth supplements doctrine, especially in the field of religious knowledge. "Every conception of the divine nature which is not contradictory and paradoxical is hopelessly far removed from the mysteries of the divine life." [1]

Now one of the living certainties in the mind of man is that man, as he appears in history, is not as God created him. And yet God did create man. How can these contradictory facts be both true? Man feels that he is the creation of God but refuses to believe that God created him as he now is, a sinful, tormented

[1] Berdyaev's *Freedom and the Spirit*, p. 72 (Bles, 1935).

being. That is the dilemma in which the Bible myth of Adam and Eve places us. That also is the essence of the doctrine of original sin. And it is to the essence of it that the General Confession looks when it says: "We have erred and strayed from Thy ways like lost sheep; we have followed too much the devices and desires of our own hearts. We have offended against Thy holy laws."

The basic sin of mankind, from which all sins follow, is, as we have already argued, the attempt to usurp God's sovereignty. In other words, it is man's effort to become his own God. Sin is not merely legal, a transgression of laws. It cannot be compared to the situation of a citizen who breaks certain laws of the state. A man who violates the laws of a state does not thereby forfeit his citizenship. He remains a citizen, however many laws he breaks, *so long as he recognises the state and its right to make laws*, whether he obeys them or not. But when he proceeds to challenge the right to power of the state, he is challenging the very foundations on which both state and law rest, and there is a qualitative difference between that action and his violations of the law. It is the difference between crime and treason. Original sin is treason in this sense. In the affirmation of his own will against God man challenges the foundations of existence and being. He tries to appropriate the power of the state itself, so to speak. He does not merely break a law, he tries to destroy the source and foundation of law. He compromises the bases of the moral order.

VI

The General Confession stresses one peculiar quality of original sin, namely, its levity, its heedlessness, its unintentionalness. "We have strayed from Thy ways like lost sheep." This expresses a very profound truth about the nature and consequence of sin, to which our contemporary situation, in particular, bears witness. How apt and precise is the word "sheep" as a figure of speech. The comparison, when expanded, makes a perfect parable of human behaviour. How do sheep get lost? They start grazing on ground familiar to them. But bit by bit they reach out for sweeter grass until at last they find themselves on land which is utterly strange. Then they bleat their forlornness. They are driven by "the devices and desires of their own hearts", by their predominating instinct to feed. As they nibble from patch to patch, they are heedless where they are going. On unfenced mountain-land, sheep stray miles away from their own pasture ground. They wander amidst great perils—bogs, precipices, ravines, poisoned herbs and so forth. All in obedience to their desire.

That is how the history of sinful man develops. It is a process in which his intentions are transformed into their opposites, or, at least, a process in which consequences assume a shape very different from original intention. Man proposes, history disposes. Egoism, whether of the individual or the group, has the knack of developing a will of its own in the interaction of events. As Engels once put it, society assumes a shape of its own, not intended by the individuals composing it. The only thing within the control of the individual is his initial act. Once that has entered into the stream of events, how it will end can no longer be perceived. That is why the road to hell is paved with good intentions—a contradiction, but a fact. Why should well-intentioned acts ever lead to evil and disaster not in the original intention? Just as the sheep might ask itself at the end of a day's most delicious grazing, when it finds itself in strange surroundings: "however did I get here?" All it has done has been to follow good grazing. It simply followed "the devices and desires of its own heart", and, unawares, it is landed in a situation for which it has no desire at all. Egocentric action—the desires of our own hearts—finally eventuates in conditions very much at variance with the individual will and desire. This profound truth is registered even in proverbs, which Lord Morley once defined as the generalisation of moral experience. "Chickens come home to roost"—but unfortunately, not as chickens. By roosting time they have been transformed into vultures, eagles or monsters. Behaviour which springs from self-centredness inevitably breeds unwanted consequences. The wine is delicious, but the subsequent headache is damnable. The human intention in original sin, in the attempt to exercise the sovereign power, which is God's alone, *always defeats itself.* That is why history is the arena of tragedy and frustration. If events remained faithful to individual

68

desire, if they adhered to the wishes of their initiators, history would have no failures to record. Instead of twenty-one civilisations ending in chaos and disintegration, there would have been one civilisation going ever "on and on and on, and up and up and up", as the late Ramsay MacDonald used to say. If obedience to "the devices and desires of our own hearts" led to the achieving of their original aim, namely, self-realisation and fulfilment, romantic lovers, for example, would never find themselves in a divorce court to expose their exhausted passions and deflated ecstasies to the gaze of the public. On the contrary, they would "live happily ever afterwards", and finally burst into unendurable bliss. They do finally burst, though not into unendurable bliss but into unendurable torment. They *stray*—and get *lost*. Here is the history of sinful man in this world.

The most dramatic and easily understood demonstration of this quality of sin is war. Its falsification of intention is obvious to the most short-sighted. War brings to the surface what is existing all the time during so-called peace. In war, a society's way of life comes to maturity. The mask is thrown off, and processes hitherto camouflaged are exposed for what they are. War is a forcing-house of social development. It demonstrates, in a more concentrated form, what is happening all the time.

War, we are told, is a gamble—which is but a succinct mode of saying that events betray the hopes of their originators. It is fairly safe guess, that when the

ex-Kaiser started the war in 1914, the very last thing
in his mind was that the end of it would be the loss of
his throne, and that he would die an exile in Doorn.
It is, if anything a still safer guess that, in his wildest
nightmare, he never envisaged the possibility that one
of his corporals would emerge to dominate Germany
and Europe: that a casual labourer would seize the
sceptre of the Hohenzollerns and succeed where he had
failed. Neither did Hitler contemplate in 1939 his own
suicide.

This process which, in war, is comprehended within
a brief period of years operates in history throughout
periods of generations and centuries. The final crystal-
lisation of an action or a policy may take hundreds of
years. We will consider, summarily, two instances.
They comprehensively illustrate the inherent character
of original sin. We will take our first example from
the Investiture Controversy.

Early in the eleventh century—1037, to be exact—
the conflict between the Empire and the Papacy came
to a head in the quarrel over the investiture of
bishops with the insignia of office. Pope Gregory
VII who was animated by an exalted zeal to reform
abuses, was determined to secure for the Church
undisturbed mastery in her own affairs, a very laudable
desire. Secular control over the Church, even when the
secular authority was religious, was an evil. After a
series of sweeping secondary changes, Gregory tackled
the problem of new episcopal institutions. Of whom
were bishops the servants and officers? Obviously the

Church; therefore the Church, in the person of the Pope, must have sole right of control over them. The Pope alone has the right to invest them into their sees. This was Gregory's claim. But the Emperor, Henry IV, challenged it on the ground that the sees into which they were instituted were feudal territories as well as ecclesiastical offices and therefore owed obligation to the Emperor as their overlord, which was anyhow a fact. In the course of his resistance to the Emperor, Gregory approached the path of claiming absolute power for the Papacy over both Church and Empire. Canossa was the thin end of the wedge—rather a thick thin-end. The Gelasian doctrine of the Two Swords[1] by which the relations between Church and Empire had hitherto been regulated, ceased to be binding. Two hundred years later, Innocent III was claiming absolute power over Church and Empire, which included the right to depose Kings and dispose of Kingdoms. What began with Gregory as a struggle to exercise power to control the Church ended with Innocent as absolute power over Church and Empire. What began as a religious reform ended as a terrible secular abuse. It transformed the Papacy into a secular despotism, masquerading as a religious authority.

[1] The doctrine of the Two Swords, known as the Gelasian Doctrine, formulated in the fifth century by Pope Gelasius I, governed the relations between Church and Empire throughout the mediaeval period; at least until the eleventh century, when Gregory VII began to upset the balance. It asserted that God had ordained the Emperor as His agent of Government in the secular sphere, and the Pope as His agent in the spiritual sphere. On the whole, it worked well. It certainly was much less of a curse to Europe than the modern doctrine of the absolute nation-state.

What began with Gregory as an attempt to bind the Church into a closer unity finally crystallised in the Reformation, which severed the Church—a situation far more disastrous both for the Church and Europe as a whole than the one Gregory had to face. It prepared the way for the growth of the sovereign nation-state, which has been a calamitous diversion of Europe from its main line of development. It tied up national freedom with localised, absolute sovereignties, a course which has immersed Europe in a continuous blood shedding. Gregory's claim for power to purify the Church finally created in the Papacy an insatiable lust for absolute power for its own sake, with the result that it so corrupted and demoralised the Papacy as to make it stink to high heaven. It was a Catholic Council that first called for the reformation of the Church "in head and members". The stubborn refusal of the Papacy to pay heed to this call made the Reformation inevitable, a disaster for the Church, but, under God, a necessary disaster, made so by a development which its initiator never intended. Gregory's intention was to effect the living unity of the Church. The forces he set in motion ultimately broke it. Whilst the later mediaeval Papacy could be more fitly compared to a beast of prey than to a sheep, its lack of insight into the psychological and spiritual significance of its lust for power was supremely sheepish. It nibbled and grabbed at power with no realisation of consequences. It strayed so far that it lost itself.

The growth of Capitalism provides us with our

second example. It started in the assertion of individual freedom and initiative. It is ending in the most soulless and brutal suppression of the individual. Let us attempt to trace the process.

Capitalism began as alternative to rigid central control of economic processes. Adam Smith, in the classic of capitalism, *The Wealth of Nations*, argued for the removal of all restraints upon trade and manufacturing at a time when those restrictions were already being broken down. The ancient feudal and mercantilist orders had become severe fetters upon trade and production. Capitalism provided the means of breaking these fetters, and production developed into a system of individual, competitive manufacturing— the production of goods for exchange in a world market. By personal initiative and enterprise individuals became prosperous and successful manufacturers.

This condition of things reflected itself in social and political theory. The individual tended to transcend society. John Locke, in 1690, formulated the doctrine of absolute individual rights, which concretely were property rights. Society existed to protect the individual in the enjoyment of those rights, and ceased to be a unity in which individuals realised their individuality by service to the community. It became a mere aggregate. The unit was the isolated individual, to whose acquisition of wealth and accumulation of property the state was subordinate. In the famous phrase of the nineteenth-century Manchester School, the duty of the state was "to keep the ring". Thus the individual, divorced from society which really made him a personality, was elevated into a position of supremacy.

In practice, this came to mean the general exploitation of the weak by the strong, of the many by the few: a minority of individuals fed their individuality on the suppression of individuality in the majority. They battened upon the miseries of the masses. And in due course, by the growth of monopoly and technology, capitalism produced a race of mechanised automata. That which originated as a protest on behalf of the individual resulted in the mechanisation and depersonalisation of the individual.

Thus we now have great commercial empires in private hands, instruments of international finance, and vast nationalised industries to which national states have committed themselves with little satisfaction to anyone. In the confusion into which the whole world has degenerated, man has lost his way completely. Capitalism which in the intentions of its pioneers was to achieve prosperity, a sort of heaven upon earth, has succeeded in creating what is more like hell. That is how original sin in man has worked its way in the modern world. What a road to travel—from individual competition to imperialist monopoly! We start with thousands of individuals fighting one another in an unregulated competitive scramble, and come to a close with a few colossi fighting for the redivision of the planet. What a theme for the tragedians of human society!

The Original Sin of Rebellion

How the avowed intention of Communism to liberate the masses from the thraldom of capitalism has resulted in a tyranny of the most complete kind we have already discussed at the opening of this book. Man's aim at liberty and justice, when taken in his own strength and with his own sight, leads him into a social state the very opposite of what he intends.

"We have erred and strayed from Thy ways like lost sheep; we have followed too much the devices and desires of our own hearts." A religious confession that has been, in the brilliant fiction of the last twenty years, a text for contemptuous mirth. It is also a concentrated description of a very grim sociology. And if we are too advanced and emancipated to pay attention to it as a religious confession, we had better give heed to it as a sociology—if we wish to survive.

VII

One of the mistakes of the eighteenth century was to regard history as a record of expanding and deepening liberty. In amplifying this romantic idea, Hegel came to the conclusion that the individual achieved maximum freedom in the absolute state. There is no idiocy beyond the capacity of great philosophers to believe. If liberty means doing what somebody else likes, there's a good deal to be said for the proposition that history is the growth of liberty, or, as Vico, the Italian philosopher put it, liberty is the "hero" of history. There is a story told of a customer who informed Henry Ford that he did not like a motor-car painted black, to which Mr. Ford replied: "My dear sir, you can have your car painted any colour you like— so long as it is black." The story is a passable parable of human history. Liberty has consisted too much in liking what somebody else wants. By following "the devices and desires of our own hearts", we become the victims of devices and desires that are not our own. By exercising his freedom to become independent of God, man has, in fact, handed himself over to necessity.

All theoretical discussion of freedom is concerned, in one way or another, with its necessary limitations— which is really contradictory. If there is restraint, there can be no liberty. If there is one thing that I refrain from doing because I am forbidden to do it, I am not free. Freedom, in the true sense, is either absolute or it is nothing. To say that in one-third of my life I am restrained, but in two-thirds I am free, is meaningless; for that is destructive of personality. True freedom is literally to be free to do what one wants. But that is impossible.

Now why? Because wants are in conflict. A's will runs counter to B's, because both A and B's desires spring out of their respective egoism. A being self-centred, and B being self-centred—that is each starts from the supremacy of his own self—conflict is inevitable. What happens in practice is that A's egoism more or less sets a check on B's, and vice versa. That is to say, A's action is partly dominated by B, and B's by A. While both A and B remain with the illusion of inward freedom—that is each considered himself to be self-determined—in fact they are inhibited and bound. A's egocentric will runs foul of B's, because both cannot be supreme. In all social life, therefore, individual action very imperfectly expresses the inner self-determined desire or will, since, at the same time, action partly frustrates it. The inner freedom is proved false by the outer necessity.

Now the only way by which inner freedom could become outer freedom, by which action could be a perfect expression of desire, would be for desires to be mutually beneficial. That is, every desire of A's should not conflict with B's but fulfil it. If what I wanted, in every single instance, you also wanted me to have or do, and everything you wanted I wanted you to have, freedom would be real. My action would then be as purely self-determined as my inner will or desire.

Now, such action is possible only if it springs from a will which is common to all individuals; if the source of desire or will is the same in everybody. If we are all dipping from the same well, we shall all be consuming the same drink. This is what St. Augustine meant in his profound saying "Love God and do as you like". If God is our common source and centre, the desires of each will be welcomed by all, and we shall participate in the actions which express them.

This was the state of man when he existed in obedience to God. Then his freedom-in-subjection was complete. Action—social relations—did not contradict will but fulfilled it. But when man departed from God, when he suffered the Fall of Man, his freedom turned into necessity. History knows nothing of real freedom, for it is a process in which inner self-determination is subject to constant frustration as it becomes external act. In history man's primal freedom has become slavery. "We have erred and strayed from Thy ways."

The symbols of man's slavery are Nature and Technics.

Until the modern era, man has been the slave of Nature, a ruthless, merciless mistress, condemning him to unremitting toil for a meagre reward. In the divine intention, man was made Lord of the world. But it would be grossly untrue to say that that has been the relation between man and Nature throughout history. Not until the triumph of technology in the last hundred years, or even less, can it be said that Nature has yielded to human will. And even now, at the moment of man's greatest victory in the conquest of the atom and the approaching conquest of space, Nature warns us that she has the winning trick up her sleeve. She has made us realise that the outcome of all our scientific discoveries and technical skills threatens to be death. Never was the extinction of man on the planet so near as today. Nature may still have the last word, which we know to be death. Nature may win in the end.

Nature's long domination of man was symbolised in poverty which, until recently, was a necessity. The wealth man extracted from Nature was utterly insufficient to release him for fuller self-realisation. Nothing limits self-determination more than poverty. And for the vast majority of mankind until today, poverty has been compulsory. The wealth produced has never been enough to enable man to use matter as the fully pliable instrument of his will. Hence his subjection to Nature of which God intended him to be master. Man's rebellion against God made him the slave of necessity. This is the dialectic of original sin.

And when, at last, by labour, imagination and creative genius, man has succeeded in fashioning an instrument, Technics, which can bend Nature to human will, that same instrument produces a new kind of political and economic slavery. Man breaks the chains which Nature riveted on his liberty of action only to discover that he has forged a new and heavier chain. Slavery to Nature resolves itself into slavery to political ideas of absolute sovereignty and their inevitable expression in forms of totalitarianism, whether disguised or not, and to economic ideas of subservience to the machine. Man's new power, Technics, has invested the egocentric will-to-power with greater potency, the greater wealth produced instead of intensifying the possibility of individual self-expression, has resulted in a new inhibition of personal will. Technics is nibbling away the inner will of men.

This is what man's satanic bid for sovereignty comes to, this is what following "the devices and desires of our own hearts" achieves. It entangles freedom—the inner self-affirmation—in the chains of slavery either to Nature or to society. The pride which drives man to challenge divine supremacy involves him in inescapable contradiction. Thus we come to confess our social sin, which is the reflection of the separation from the love of God in which our individual hearts are involved.

Three

THE NEGATIVE AND THE POSITIVE CHARACTER OF SIN

"We have left undone those things which we ought to have done, and have done those things which we ought not to have done."

I

THIS ASSERTION COULD MOST TRULY SERVE AS THE epitaph of every human being. At the end of every life, be it short or long, when the earthly accounts are finally summed up, this sombre, humbling fact stands out—the things which ought to have been done were left undone, and things which ought not to have been done were done, in profusion. Not one of the myriads of the men and women that have passed through this vale of tears—with one exception—could truthfully say at the journey's end: "My life was made up only of the things I ought to have done; amongst them was not a single one which I ought not to have done." *In this matter*, saint and sinner; good and bad are all on the same level. There is no democracy like the democracy of sin. Its equalitarianism is perfect and absolute.

Now this is a staggering fact, is it not? *What can be*

the matter with human nature? Let the reader dwell on this universal fact. However good a human being may become—and we have record of some peerless achievements in goodness—he never quite escapes the fatality of conscience. Right to the very end, even at the rare ethereal summit of saintliness, there are things done which ought not to have been done. Something radically, disastrously wrong somewhere in human nature!

This profound individual failure is reflected in social life. Every civilisation is the same in this, that it has done the things it ought not, and left undone the things it ought. It is in the social aspect of this fundamental human failure that the unbearable stupidity and irrationality of man assumes such gigantic proportions as to be beyond the capacity of the most romantic rationalist to deny. Governments, classes and corporations neglect the most elementary necessities and perform the most extreme idiocies. It reveals the cruel contradiction in which collective humanity involves itself: by failing to do the obviously wise and elementary thing, it lands itself in a situation in which there is absolutely no escape from the doing of the most stupid and the most irrational things. Let us confine our examples to our own Western civilisation. Destruction of wealth has always been a feature of capitalist society. Witness the recurrent depressions of world-trade—in the nineteenth century every ten years or so. But never until the late 'twenties and early 'thirties of our century did it become the deliberate aim of governments and commercial combinations. Foods and raw materials were destroyed in colossal quantities at a time when masses of people in advanced industrial countries—to say nothing of the peasantry in backward countries—were undernourished precisely for the lack of these goods. What could be more stupid or immoral than to pour milk down drains by the thousand gallons, when children by the hundred thousand were half starving for the lack of it? The tale of the great holocaust is too familiar for repetition—the burnt coffee of Brazil; the burnt wheat of Canada and the U.S.A.; the burnt carcasses of the Argentine; the fish thrown back into the sea; the Dutch East Indies supplies of quinine wantonly destroyed, and so on.

In the same period, politics came to the aid of capitalist organisation in the task of damming the tide of wealth production. Here in Britain we had the series of Marketing Board Acts for the deliberate restriction of production; there were European Wheat Conferences to cut down the supplies of wheat and other cereals. In the U.S.A. there were the gigantic contradictions of the New Deal legislature. President Roosevelt spent millions of dollars to subsidise idle farmers. Stock breeders were paid for not growing stock. Wheat farmers, cotton farmers, tobacco growers, were all paid in accordance with the amount of crops which they agreed *not* to cultivate. The things which ought not to have been done were the things done—and with a vengeance. When millions were crying out for bread, wheat was burnt in loco-motives and furnaces.

Now these and other monstrous idiocies were not done for the fun of the thing. Statesmen and captains of finance and industry, whatever their actual short-comings, were not perverted monsters indulging them-selves in sadistic super-orgies, though such wholesale destruction was supremely the activity of Neronian perversity. Strange as it may seem, these destructive policies and pursuits had become relatively necessary as the consequences of not doing "what we ought to have done". "By leaving undone those things which we ought to have done," we were driven to the point of doing the things we ought not to do. The negative character of sin leads to a positive situation of wrong-doing, which refuses to fit into the formulas of the simple moralist.

The wholesale destruction of wealth in the post-war years was symptomatic of a profound crisis in capitalist society. The contradiction between a socialised process of production and an individual, private process of wealth appropriation had become too intense to permit any further social progress. What, therefore, *ought* to have been done was a revolutionary, reorganisation of society by which production of wealth should become directly, consciously subordinated to personal, general consumption. It would have meant a drastic inter-ference with private vested interests. This was the essential, summary task which the post-war world ought to have done.

That was after the First World War; the situation repeated itself after the Second World War. At the present day, the great undisposable stocks of wheat are one of the most serious problems of United States economy. That astounding fact is only one of the examples of the inability of men in society to attain balance in their economy.

The failure even to attempt this balance, with the partial exception of Russia, in anything but financial terms, leaves us still in the utter irrationality of being unable to cope with our vast economic potentialities. "We have left undone the things which we ought to have done, and have done the things which we ought not to have done." Between the "not doing" of the one thing and the "doing" of the other there is a profound organic connection—a connection which entangles mankind in an inescapable contradiction. And as by a relentless fatality Europe staggered and reeled, for a generation like a drunken man, from one disaster to another, until, at last, it became involved in the gigantic calamity of total war, which intensified to the nth degree the destructive character of a capitalism no longer capable of serving the ends of social progress, so now the whole world is in terror of the self-destructive capacity of a self-centred humanity in nuclear war.

II

Sin is man's "No" to God, and history is the sphere in which the human denial of God's will operates.

The "No", however, consists of the positive assertion of egocentric will as against God. Man's "No" is not mere passive negation, but a denial which takes the positive form of the affirmation of human will as supreme, so that sin is both negative and positive. The positive is the necessary consequence of the prior negative. We leave undone the things we ought to do. The negative involves the positive. History is not a vacuum, in which, having denied the will of God, we can remain in a passive inertness. Man says "No" to God by saying "Yes" to himself. This fact has two or three most important implications.

First, sin is not mere negation, not just absence of light. It is a tension of both negation and affirmation. Sin is not mere defect, to which so much of Liberal Protestant theology reduced it. Here, as in other fields of modern thought, Hegelianism laid its distorting hand. History is a process of the self-realisation of the Absolute—a profoundly anti-Biblical, anti-Christian view. Thus sin becomes merely a discarded "moment" in the dialectical process by which Absolute Spirit moves to fulfilment from thesis to antithesis. Such a concept deprives sin of its fatal element of guilt, of personal responsibility—that element which says "thou art the man". It becomes a "missing of the mark", an idea which the Greek word *hamartano* encourages. The sinner thus becomes simply a slightly inferior marksman. He is aiming all the time at the target. He merely fails to hit it to a greater or less degree. Sin, therefore, is merely failure.

But sin is much more than this. "We have left *undone* . . ." There is a radical, fatal deliberate will at work. The sinner is not merely an inefficient marksman. He is a deliberate perverse marksman. Instead of aiming at the target, he deliberately chooses another target of his own—and hits it every time. Sin is not a slight deviation from a main line of development which is leading straight to the Kingdom of Heaven. It is itself the main line of development leading in exactly the opposite direction. It is more than error. It is a deliberate persistence in self-chosen wrong. It is only in so far as sin has this positive element that we can speak of guilt at all. And it is precisely guilt that constitutes the tragedy and sinfulness of sin. To speak of guilt in connection with mere failure or mistake is meaningless. We don't say that a child who makes a mistake, for example in arithmetic, is guilty. Careless or slip-shod—but not guilty. But when a child is *disobedient*, when it deliberately goes its own way, contrary to expressed will, then it is guilty. In all sin, therefore, there is a positive affirmation of will in disobedience to another Will. We leave undone what we ought to have done, because we choose to do what we ought not to do.

Secondly—and this is an expansion of the preceding discussion—a sin is not a blundering quest for the will and purpose of God. Many years ago, the Rev. R. J. Campbell, who was minister of the City Temple at the time, made himself notorious by saying that the *roué*, in his lustful and drunken activities, was really seeking for God. To continue the analogy, all the crimes and tragedies and iniquities that make up history's cruel tale are but the tragic errors of a race of god-seekers—which is to reduce history and reason to a madhouse. The cynical blasphemies and obscene cruelties of Cesare Borgia, on this reasoning, are reduced to a search for God, even though perverted.

The only sense in which it can be said that man's sinful affirmations of himself are a quest for God is that they are endeavours to seek the satisfaction, the fulfilment, of the craving in his nature which his denial of God has created. Rebellion against God has opened a vacuum in human nature. Nature abhors the vacuum in soul no less than in the material universe. "Our hearts are restless till they rest in Thee." That vacuum must be filled, if not by God, then by the devil of self. All the lusts and excesses of human behaviour are attempts to satisfy that "aching void the world can never fill". That is why all human interests and passions, without exception, are of only temporary capacity to satisfy, in so far as they are expressions of self-will—round holes for square pegs. The character of these passions makes no difference. They may be gross, like drunkenness or sexual lust; they may be refined, like a passion for music or poetry or art. It is no accident that it is among artists that we often find the wildest excesses of behaviour. Man, as a result of his fall from Divine Grace, is cursed by an infinite craving, which nothing can satisfy for long. In this sense, indeed, man is searching for God in his sin—but only in this sense.

The Negative and the Positive Character of Sin

But man is seeking satisfaction in and from himself. That is the basic fact about human behaviour and history, which no romantic sentimentalism should be allowed to obscure for one moment. Men may, and do, of course, rationalise their motives and aims. They seek to hide from themselves their own deepest knowledge—that they are bent on their own will-to-power at whatever cost. Even Hitler had to persuade himself—not merely the German people and the world, but himself, and himself most of all—that his lust for power was somehow identified with Providence. The very fact of psychological rationalisation is profoundly significant. It is a proof of man's deep awareness of guilt, that he is denying God, deliberately—more deliberately and fanatically than he is doing anything else. Why rationalise what isn't there? Why does the soul try to persuade itself that its motives are other than they are in reality, if the knowledge of what they are in their nakedness is something that he dare not face? The process of rationalisation, which modern psychology has shown to be a basic characteristic of human mind, is certain proof that man wills self to the exclusion of aught else. There is no escape from responsibility before God by the attempt to persuade oneself that in pursuing self-will, one is really seeking for God. We leave undone the things of God in order that we may do the things we desire.

Thus history is a real drama of real conflicting wills. It is not an illusion. It is not an elaborate stage-play in which men are puppets nursing the delusion of freedom, and where everything is sure to come right in the end. Human freedom is a grim and awful reality. There is, therefore, no *guarantee* that everything will turn out right in the end. The reality of freedom carries with it the satanic possibility that men may choose to go on defying God. Our hope is in the infinite will of God which is determined to suffer and to endure and to love man into willing submission to Himself. By faith, that hope may become a spiritual equivalent of certainty, but *not automatic*. Man is a free agent, not a puppet. Hence, history is real.

From negation of God to affirmation of self—here is the dynamic progression of man as sinner. Man derives from God's creative act and will. Man, therefore, is conscious first of God, then of himself as related to God. Sin begins in the negation of the primary awareness of God—then it becomes affirmation of the derivatory, the secondary, the created will. Sin is the deliberate attempt to kill God.

Four

THE CORRUPTION OF HUMAN NATURE

"And there is no health in us."

NO STATEMENT IN THE WHOLE RANGE OF CHRISTIAN
theology constitutes so mortal an offence or so uncompromising a challenge to human self-esteen as
this assertion that there is no health or soundness in
human nature. Nothing is more destructive of pride.
Man is corrupt, or rather, tends to turn corrupt. Man
is also dynamic, and in the course of his development
the rottenness which lies at the core of his being inevitably and necessarily reveals itself. This is the one
thing which human pride will not accept. Not only
will it not accept it. It will not even consider it. It does
not penetrate our sociology even as a possibility. In
all our sociology, with the single exception of the
Catholic, the one assumption which is never argued
or discussed is the unquestioned capacity of human
nature for complete achievement and self-realisation.
All secular sociology is built on that silent hypothesis.
In their attitude to the Christian assertion of the
corruption of human nature, sociologists flout the
primary premises of their science (*sic*)![1] All of which

[1] R. Niebuhr's *Christianity and Power Politics*, p. 36 (Scribners, 1940). " 'If

is evidence of the desperate character of human pride, which will resort to any device to escape the Christian challenge to human nature.

The primary and obvious form which human reaction to the Christian challenge takes is complete denial of what seems to be one of its implications. And this, no doubt, conceals a genuine difficulty. To affirm that man is corrupt seems to argue that he is incapable of performing any good deed or achieving any condition of goodness. In other words, to say that man is corrupt is merely another way of stating the doctrine of total depravity; that the natural man— man as he is in history—cannot do any good thing. To discover that human corruption means total depravity is a great relief to the natural man; for it makes any further consideration of it unnecessary. Total depravity is so plainly at variance with the facts that the Christian challenge can be dismissed without further ado.

It certainly is contrary to all human experience, and is therefore not true. If Christianity depends on the total depravity of human nature, then it has no significance for the world, except as a museum piece. The humanist contention that people on the whole are very decent

we can find the real cause of social injustice,' said a typical modern recently, 'we should be forced to go back to the absurd doctrine of original sin.' That remark is a revelation of the scientific 'objectivity' of modernity. The Christian idea of original sin is ruled out *a priori*. That is understandable enough in a non-Christian world. What is absurd is that modern Christianity should have accepted this modern rejection of the doctrine of original sin with such pathetic eagerness, and should have spent so much energy in seeking to prove that a Christian can be just as respectable and modern as a secularist."

and kindly can be acknowledged without difficulty. They really are. The behaviour of the British people under aerial bombardment, for example, was truly magnificent, and justly earned the admiration of the U.S.A. and all neutral countries.

But the General Confession does not teach total depravity. "There is no health in us" does not mean "man is incapable of any goodness". Total depravity was the desperate and perverse reaction of scholastic Protestantism to the self-deification of man in the Enlightenment and Romance of the eighteenth century. It was orthodoxy in a state of panic. What began in the fifteenth-century Renaissance as a modest assertion of human self-sufficiency had become, in eighteenth-century Enlightenment, a confident, overweening pride. The tiny rill of consciousness of human greatness had swollen into a roaring river of human omnipotence. The doctrine of total depravity was a desperate, semi-conscious attempt to stem the flood of human arrogance and *hubris*. It was the reaction of a theology lacking in science to a science lacking in theology.

What, then, does the General Confession mean when it affirms that "there is no health in us"?

It means that man is unsound, diseased, in the deep root of his being; that right at the core of his ego, there is a fatal poison and perversity, which seeps into all his behaviour and social institutions. "There is a maggot in the apple." It is this central perversity in man which reduces to futility and failure all his historic efforts

93

at civilisation and utopia. It is the same perversity which makes it impossible for man to achieve happiness and self-fulfilment and social harmony. Try as he will—and man has made some magnificent efforts throughout the centuries—he always fails; and always will fail. The most promising ventures, at some point or other of their development, turn upon themselves in frustration and self destruction. As Nietzsche's Zarathustra said: "Verily, a polluted stream is man." This is the ultimate fact of unredeemed man in history.

"And there is no health in us" is the final religious fact underlying man's whole historical development. It is the principle of the most fundamental law of history, if by "law" is meant the statement of what always happens. This law may be formulated as follows; *every good achieved by the natural man is negated by a corresponding evil.* Every gain becomes a loss. Every problem solved by man only gives rise to a greater problem. Human progress consists in finding new forms for old evils. All human solutions are temporary.

This, in fact, is what has happened throughout the 6,000 years of the history of civilised man, up to the present. And the prospect for anything different for the future is, to put it modestly, not rosy. This fundamental historic law demonstrates one thing above all else: *that it is beyond the power of collective man to save himself from the fate which dogs and dooms all his efforts.* We will consider some examples of the working of this law in history, politics, science and psychology.

The Corruption of Human Nature

Throughout his 6,000 years of history, civilised man has undergone many changes in his environment and also in himself. In changing his environment, he has also changed himself. It has been an interesting process. The change has been twofold.

First, it has been an increase in man's powers over his surroundings; and, second, with that increase, a growth in the complexity of the environment. There is obviously a tremendous difference between the early food-gatherers and modern European man. The food-gatherer was *constantly* at the mercy of Nature. Modern man is only ultimately at the mercy of Nature, in virtue of the fact that death squares the whole account. The vast technical achievement of man in civilisation is partly the result, partly the cause, of a greater inner development also. The range and depth of modern man's consciousness is very much wider and deeper. He knows more; he feels more intensely; he lives more complicatedly. His powers both in his interior and exterior life are infinitely greater.

But, deeper than all these changes in consciousness and technique, man's fundamental nature has remained unaltered. The more he has changed, the more indeed has he remained the same. The parrot cry of the political reactionary that "you can never change human nature" is tragically true, though in a much profounder sense than he realises. What the reactionary is arguing is that you should not attempt to alter the social and political institutions through which human nature expresses itself. What the Christian doctrine of human corruption states is that throughout all the changes in social forms—which are necessary and unavoidable—human nature itself persists fundamentally the same. And that is man's supreme tragedy. The outer body of humanity—its systems and civilisations —distintegrates and then renews itself. But the inner man, the deep, hard core of spirit and being continues unaltered. The things in which the ancient Egyptian, for example, and modern Western man differ, in spite of their spectacular magnitude, are not as significant as that in which they are at one—their egocentric will and mind. This persistent self-will is demonstrated by the inevitable process of self-destruction in which all civilisations seem to be involved.

The staggering fact about all human history is this: *that every effort at creating a continuously-progressive, growing civilisation has hitherto failed.* After 6,000 years of trying, man is further from succeeding than ever. His accumulating experience, contrary to all logic and common sense, only makes his failure more gigantic and tragic.

We have record of twenty-one civilisations.[1] These are: Egyptian, Andean, Sinic, Minoan, Sumerian, Mayan, Syriac, Indic, Hittite, Hellenic, Arabic, Iranian, Hindu, Mexican, Yucatec, Babylonian, Orthodox Christian (in Russia), Orthodox Christian (out-

[1] Arnold J. Toynbee, *A Study of History* (Oxford University Press). My obligations to this work are immeasurable.

side Russia), Far Eastern (in Japan and Korea), Far Eastern (main body outside Japan), and last, but not least, our Western civilisation. These represent the twenty-one attempts of civilised man to make a going concern of organised social life on the basis of egocentric will. Or, in other words, they are the twenty-one attempts to make a success of systematic living, independently of God. And the profoundly significant thing about them is *that every one of them is a complete and utter failure.* The more grandiose the attempt, the more colossal and disastrous the failure. Man has succeeded in not succeeding.

Now of these twenty-one civilisations, fourteen are moribund. They have completely dissolved into the dust and silence of eternity. So utterly dead are some of them, that even their one-time existence was unknown until a few years ago, when the patient labour of the archaeologist brought them to light. These mighty monuments that aspired to eternity left hardly a trace behind them. These few traces, so laboriously unearthed, tell us little more than that such societies existed once upon a time. Various causes combined to wreck them. Their many social forms and institutions, to which so much labour and suffering and tragedy were concentrated, were destroyed, thus necessitating a fresh start. It is forever impossible to calculate the consequent waste of experience and effort.

Thus for the twenty-one experiments in ordered living how many remain? Apart from the Hindu and the Islamic and our Western civilisation, are there any?

97

The Orthodox Church exists, but its civilisation has been revolutionised into its opposite in every country in which it existed; in the Far East, a total transformation of ancient civilisations is in rapid progress. And our Western civilisation, including Europe, the Americas and some countries of the British Commonwealth, is in peril, for its capitalist basis and democracy are both challenged. Before the coming of capitalism, civilisations existed on the planet as independent entities. The breakdown of one did not involve that of the rest. There was always a refuge somewhere on the face of the earth for ordered, progressive living; so, at one and the same time, a society was in the throes of disintegration, whilst another was experiencing the pains of growth. Mankind was made up of several societies. But for weal and woe, capitalism welded humanity into a single society or collective. By its creation of a world-market, capitalism bought about an inter-relationship between the most primitive, backward races and the most advanced peoples. Primitive Africa is interlocked with modern Europe in a vast planetary common existence. At long last civilisation has no further refuge from the barbarian. The barbarian is now everywhere within the frontiers. That is why isolation is the ludicrous dream of Rip Van Winkles. Science has destroyed the last rampart between civilisation and barbarism. Humanity is now a single society.

Our Western civilisation faces the uprising national consciousness of Africa and Asia, which challenges not only our capitalistic control, which it throws off, but the basic assumptions of our democratic institutions, which it refuses to accept. This is the grim situation in which mankind finds itself, after millennia of striving and suffering. The fate of one will be the fate of all. The internal aspect of this was the erasure in the last war of the distinction between combatant and non-combatant. Just as history unified societies externally, so it is also unifying them internally. To attempt to preserve the artificial social and economic distinctions between people, in face of the overwhelming unifying force of historic development, is as pathetic and futile as Canute's effort to stay the incoming tide. Men must flow with that tide or be engulfed.

Now, the basic fact in our time is that we are witnessing the end of our Western civilisation.

Thus of the twenty-one experiments in social independence of God, which is, theologically, what a civilisation means, not one has been a success. Each has created more problems than it could solve. The very solutions it effected gave rise to new and insoluble problems. The process itself is radically contradictory. The means by which a particular civilisation solves its problem, or rather that of its predecessor, is also the means by which it creates the problem it cannot solve. The dilemma which eventually breaks it is taken over by the new succeeding civilisation. But in resolving the dilemma of the old, the new breeds a new dilemma. And so on—but not *ad infinitum*. That process has a limit, and the profound question to which the present crisis of the West gives rise is *whether that limit has not already been reached.* Now that mankind has been made by science and the march of political powers into the elements of a single collective, has it reached the position in which it can no longer do what has previously been done: shuffle over its insoluble problem on to a world civilisation? In history, which came to adolescence during the period we call Ancient, and reached maturity in the period we designate Modern, is mankind now entering its phase of senility? Senility is a phase in which the balance between the katabolic process and the anabolic is disturbed. The katabolic, disintegrating process gains at the expense of the anabolic, renewing process, which ultimately ends in death. Has the long tragic grandeur of man's story now entered into the twilight of irremediable decline?

Whatever the answer to this grave question, it is at least clear that our existing civilisation is being destroyed by the problems of its own making, the solution of which is proving to be beyond its power. The Nation State, by means of which capitalism transcended the deadlock of Feudalism, has grown into an all-consuming Frankenstein, whose insatiable appetite demands all the hard-won gains of civilised man. It has met its opposite, which is multiplying in strength and capacity, and is seeking to solve this problem of civilisation by abolishing civilisation itself, by going forward to a new barbarism, which, of course, it calls by another name, borrowed from Christian lore; but in the process, it is making personality impossible.

Now this tremendous, terrible fact—that every attempt at civilisation ends in self-destructive failure—should certainly raise the question: what's wrong with human nature? It should, let me repeat, at least *raise* the question. The man who can view this calamitous repetition in human history without being driven to ask himself whether there isn't something wrong with human nature must be in a bad way. If he thinks at all, he cannot avoid it. The question becomes still more insistent when we come to understand *how* successive civilisations have failed.

Let us turn again to the testimony of Dr. Arnold Toynbee. "Our inquiry into the cause of the breakdown of civilisation has led us, so far, to a succession of negative conclusions. We have found that these breakdowns are not acts of God. They are neither the operations of a Saeva Necessitas, nor the sadistic sport of a Kali snatching another bead for her necklace of skulls. Nor are they the vain repetitions of senseless laws of Nature, like the monotonous revolutions of the Earth round its own axis and of the Planets round the Sun . . . We have found, again, that we cannot legitimately attribute these breakdowns to a loss of command over the environment, either physical or human. The breakdowns of civilisations are not catastrophes of the same order as famines and floods and tornadoes and fires and shipwrecks and railway accidents; and they are not the equivalent, in the experience of bodies social, of mortal injuries inflicted in homicidal assault."[1]

This disposes of the easy assumption that the failure of civilisation is due to some cause operating completely outside the sphere of human will or control. On the contrary, purely external factors, like the physical environment, seem to be favourable to the success of civilisations rather than to their breakdown. Even when it is unfavourable, indeed, especially when it is unfavourable, it stimulates man to his greatest triumphs. The effect of external blows and pressure upon man has been to call forth new creative powers. "And the evidence, so far as it goes, suggests that . . . an increase in command over the environment was a concomitant of breakdown and distintegration and not of growth."[2] That is, precisely when man's *technical* power was increasing, his *moral* power was decreasing. Man, therefore, is not the helpless victim of some diabolical, brutal external force or power, which, like some sadist, waits till the child has completed building its house of bricks, and then kicks it down. Whatever the cause, it does not lie outside the sphere of human will and mind. Let Dr. Toynbee continue.

"Thus the increasing command over the environment which an ironic or malicious or retributive Providence is apt to bestow upon a society in disintegration only serves, in the end, to put a greater driving power into the suicidally demented society's chosen work of

[1] *A Study of History*, Vol. IV pp. 119-20.   [2] Ibid., Vol. V, p. 15.

self-destruction; and the story turns out to be a simple illustration of the theme that 'the wages of sin is death'. Our criterion for the process of the disintegration of a civilisation has to be sought elsewhere; and the clue is given to us in the spectacle of that division and discord within the bosom of a society to which an increase in its command over the environment can so often be traced back. This is only what we should expect; for we have found already that the ultimate criterion and the fundamental cause of the breakdown of civilisation is an outbreak of internal discord through which they forfeit their faculty of self-determination." [1]

Internal discord! The failure is thus traceable to human nature, so some cause that has its seat in the heart and will of man. Now why? However can you account for the fact that *every time* it is man himself that destroys the work of his own hands except by saying that there's something wrong at the roots of his being that "there is no health in us?" It is not a failure of intelligence in the technical sense. As Dr. Toynbee amply proves, it is when intelligence is at its highest, as exercised in maximum control over the environment, that man's radical perversity is most active.

On the basis of egocentric will, all societies are doomed to self-destruction, be the process long or short. This self-will is the fundamental disease of humanity. All man's advice and progress make not the

[1] *A Study of History*, Vol. V, pp. 16–17.

slightest difference to the nature or character of self-centred will, except to make it more efficient and dynamic in its self-destructive function. Modern man is incomparably more self-destructive than mediaeval or ancient man. And his successor will be more destructive still. "We know enough to be sure that the scientific achievements of the next fifty years will be far greater, more rapid and more surprising than those we have already experienced. The slide-lathe enabled machines of precision to be made, and the power of steam rushed out upon the world. And through the steam clouds flashed the dazzling lightning of electricity. But this is only a beginning. High authorities tell us that new sources of power, vastly more important than any we yet know, will surely be discovered." [1] What use will self-centred man make of such new powers? It is too ghastly to contemplate!

This fear of the future is speculative. But about the past and the present there is nothing speculative. It is all too grimly concrete and positive. In twenty-one attempts to create a stable society, subject to a continuous growth and progress, man has failed every time. The conclusion we draw is that there must be something or other in the heart or being of man which precludes him from ever succeeding with the nature—self-centred will—with which he has operated hitherto. One does not need a theological training to make that inference. It is just plain common sense.

[1] Winston Churchill, *Thoughts and Adventures*, p. 274 (Thornton Butterworth). This book was first published in November, 1932.

Let us turn now to the more specific field of political development, and more particularly of democracy. A consideration of the growth of democracy will also show the law of corruption at work, the law which ordains that the good which man achieves is negated by the evil which that good itself creates. And first of all let us indicate what we mean by democracy.

There is considerable confusion in the minds of people about the exact meaning of the word. Some think of democracy as an affirmation of human equality, in which case the stoics were democrats. Others confuse democracy with mere electoral devices, like majority voting, second ballot, proportional representation, etc. Whilst these and other ideas may be elements in the general concept of democracy, we have to seek a more exact definition.

By democracy we mean a society in which responsibility for the government of that society is an obligation resting upon all its adult members, without any distinction of sex or social status. That is what democracy is, specifically and concretely, as distinct from its idealistic background, or religious and philosophical foundations. Since this is so, it is obvious that democracy is a modern product. It is absurd, for instance, to call Athens a democracy, when nearly two-thirds of its population consisted of slaves. Democracy can be called a modern product only in the sense that it began as a process in modern Europe, not that it has been anywhere completely established. It began as a process in the struggle against Charles I. When Hampden and Pym insisted that there should be "no taxation without representation", they initiated the modern revolution, which has since undergone many great changes. The democratic tide steadily advanced from the Puritan struggle to the American Declaration of Independence; thence to the French Revolution and the growth of democracy throughout the nineteenth century, until the First World War, after which the tide receded, and reaction violently brought about the Second World War; and despite its victory, democracy is today fighting for its very existence.

Now the achievement of democracy is one of the greatest, if not the greatest, gains of the natural man. It is unquestionably a great human good, and even Marxist Communism claims to advance it. That every adult bears equal responsibility for the government of his society is a great idea. And the embodiment of that idea in the structure of society is even greater. The idea of democracy is a reflection in history of the relations between individuals in the Kingdom of Heaven. Let the reader note well what I am saying here. It is a *reflection*—and reflections always distort. It is, moreover, a reflection of the relations between *individuals*—not between the individual and God. That relation is not at all democratic. God is not a sort of Prime Minister, the chief representative of a gorgeous humanity. The relation between God and the individual is beyond understanding. We are His ministers, we are intended to represent Him, and because we owe Him our being we owe Him our entire, unqualified loyalty. We are His, not our own, not society's. To be the slave of God is our highest glory. The Kingdom of God is a community in which all individuals are wholly subordinate to Him, and by reason of that relationship are equal with one another. Democracy is an inverted attempt to realise that relation (mutual social equality) as a legislative, institutional, compulsive thing. It is an attempt to create artificially what is, in the divine order, a spontaneous, inner purposed, relationship. Democracy in heaven is an ecstatic reality. On earth it is a laborious, clumsy objective. But even such democracy as is now in historic development is probably the noblest good which unredeemed man has yet realised, and worth all the tragedy and mortal suffering called for by its defence.

Yet democracy is the source of the greatest evil too. This greatest good and gain of man has also brought the greatest evil in its train. It has transformed war from an aristocratic pastime into an arena of universal destruction and savagery.

Universal peace has been the rosy dream of some of the greatest democratic thinkers and statesmen. It must be admitted that their diagnosis of war was very shallow, as shallow as that of the socialists who attribute war to capitalism, which, they say, is the root of war. How many eloquent speeches have been made on that theme! And in an earlier generation, men made equally eloquent speeches on absolutist monarchy as a root of war. Kings and princes were the cause of war. Abolish them, give the people power—and war would be no more. Richard Cobden, with the peculiar optimism that seemed to characterise the Manchester School, envisaged the abolition of war as the result of buying in the cheapest market and selling in the dearest. What a colossal rationalisation of self-interest! Universal Free Trade would mean Universal Peace. The People don't want war. As though not wanting a thing is a guarantee that you won't get it! When Tennyson looked into the future "far as human eye could see"— he must have been short-sighted—he saw "the Parliament of man and the federation of the world".

> *When the war-drums throbbed no longer*
> *And the battle-flags were furled.*

Democracy would mean the ending of war. It was going to be as easy as that. Let Dick, Tom and Harry and Mary Jane have power, and the world would swim in the milk of human kindness. Let us see what has actually happened.

The absolutist, despotic society, in which the struggle for democracy took its rise, was one in which war was "the sport of kings and princes". War, of course, is always an evil, but in pre-democratic societies, at least, it did not involve the whole of social life. It was severely restricted to the professional combatants. It was a profession for the soldier as well as for the officer. Kings hired their soldiers wherever they could get them to fight their battles, and shortage of money was but one of many factors that kept their ambitions within bounds. This resulted in many ironic situations. Protestant Englishmen fought for French and Spanish Catholic kings. Popes hired sturdy Dutch Protestants to wage their wars. Many of the celebrated Gustav's soldiers in the Thirty Years War were Catholics. In pre-democratic Europe it was not peoples but kings and dynasties that went to war with what soldiers they could hire. The people, i.e. the peasant, the craftsman, the merchant, the scholar, continued the even tenor of their ways mostly undisturbed.

One consequence of this was that war was conducted with a certain chivalry and professional decency. At the battle of Fontenoy, in the war of the Austrian Succession, when the English Guards came into contact at last with the French Guards, an English officer stepped out of the ranks and, bowing towards the French, said: "French Guards, will you please fire first." Can one imagine that happening today? When the battle was over, and the question who was the victor, who the vanquished, had been satisfactorily settled, they all shook hands, and, so to speak, had a drink. In 1783, when France defeated Britain, the British possession of Canada was left undisturbed, even though the colony had been barely ceded. As late as 1859, after the battle of Solferino, Emperor Francis Joseph of ill-starred fame, remarked philosophically: "Ah well! I have lost a battle, I will pay with a province." Eighty years later, Marshal Pétain thought he could do the same with Hitler, that he could pay for a lost war with a province. But eighty years of progress about which modern optimism had grown so lyrically dithyrambic, marked a great step forward in savagery and lust for power, and France had to pay for a time with nearly half her country, then virtually with the whole.

A second consequence of the pre-democratic restriction of war was the greater regard for the civilian population, which is in so marked a contrast to the present. War today is waged primarily against the civilian. That is, there are no civilians any more when it comes to war. In the seventeenth and eighteenth centuries there were certain well-defined and observed customs of war.

(*a*) Towns were hardly ever wrecked by bombardment. "Several of the cities and towns of the present Franco-Belgian Frontier region were repeatedly besieged in the wars of the eighteenth century, but their great churches and cathedrals of the Middle Ages remained intact. This is true also of their town halls and numbers of their old houses. The civil population had to endure shortness of food in a siege and ran serious danger after a storm, but a bombardment of churches and homes as a means of accelerating surrender is 'a modern improvement'." [1]

(*b*) In other ways, also, the civilian population were spared to a far greater extent than in later wars. "In the record of eighteenth-century campaigns, there

[1] *European Civilisation*, Vol. V, pp. 1087-1260. Edited by Edward Eyre (Oxford University Press, 1937).

are what seem to us strange instances of long delays in arranging for the use of supplies accumulated on the spot till leave has been secured from the civil authorities." [1]

It is a strange paradox that the democratic intensification of war is at the expense of the democracy itself. Kings when they made war, spared the people, but the people, when they make war, spare nobody, not even themselves. Is this an obscure and dark exemplification of the Freudian wish-to-die?

Pre-democratic society, then, restricted warfare within narrow limits and practised some humanity in its wars. "Happy eighteenth century, which had only human weapons, small forces and limited funds at its command in warfare ... Restricted warfare was one of the loftiest achievements of the eighteenth century. It belongs to the class of hot-house plants which can only thrive in an aristocratic and qualitative civilisation. We are no longer capable of it. It is one of the fine things which we have lost as a result of the French Revolution." [2]

Democracy, giving to every man some stake in the country, has increased the evil of war beyond measure. It first of all created conscription, for it was democratic France, not despotic Prussia, that first introduced it (though the national war of liberation waged by Prussia with conscript troops was very popular); but by the institution of the *levée-en-masse*, revolutionary

[1] Ibid., p. 1110.
[2] Ferreo, *War and Peace*, quoted by Dr. Toynbee in *A Study of History*, Vol. IV, p. 150.

France prepared the first steps of the way which led, about one hundred and fifty years later, to Totalitarian Germany. The French National Assembly in 1790 was intoxicated with the new wine of democracy, but Mirabeau warned them. His licentious dissipations did not cloud his prophetic vision. "Hearken to me, all free peoples. Listen all free assemblies. You will become famous for the greater ambitiousness of your wars, and for the greater barbarity with which you will fight them." The first article in the Draft Law introducing conscription read: "Single men will fight in the front line. Married men will make the arms and munitions and man the supply services. The women will make the uniforms and serve in the hospitals. Children will assist the women by measuring and cutting the cloth. And old men will harangue the masses, and preach hatred of kings so as to unite free peoples." The deputies of the Assembly were so carried away by the reading of this that they demanded an encore, and Barras had to read it a second time. Deluded fools! They thought they were destroying tyranny, when in fact they were preparing a new tyranny compared with which the despotism of Louis XVI was a blessing.

Democracy has created the psychological and spiritual conditions in which war can become, literally, the destroyer of the human race, just as science has created the technical means. Science has produced the tools for the job; democracy has produced the will to use them, even in spite of its desire not to do so—a fact which deepens the contradiction. Natural man's greatest good thus turns into greatest evil. "The organisation of mankind into great States and Empires and the rise of nations to full collective consciousness enabled enterprises of slaughter to be planned and executed upon a scale and with a perseverance never before imagined. All the noblest virtues of individuals were gathered together to strengthen the destructive capacity of the mass. Good finances, the resources of world-wide credit and trade, the accumulation of large capital reserves, made it possible to divert for considerable periods the energies of whole peoples to the task of Devastation. Democratic institutions gave expression to the will-power of millions . . . Mankind has never been in this position before. Without having improved appreciably in virtue or enjoying wiser guidance, it has got into its hands for the first time the tools by which it can unfailingly accomplish its own extermination. That is the point in human destinies to which all the glories and toils of men have at last led them." [1]

This process of the democratic transformation of war into universal destruction began with the French Revolution. And in the name of freedom, the French masses supported Napoleon in his wars of conquest. For nearly fifteen years, Napoleon was enabled to dominate Europe with the enthusiastic consent of the French democracy. Fifty years later, another Napoleon also secured the democratic support of France for

[1] Winston Churchill's *Thoughts and Adventures*, pp. 246–8.

glory and conquest. But the profound contradiction in democracy is not a popular lust for aggrandisement; for that may prove to be temporary, like measles in children. The contradiction lies in the fact that *precisely out of the moral development of the people there issues a new immorality*. It was the widespread passion for political freedom in the masses—surely a good thing— that changed the chivalry of dynastic wars into the deadly hatred and brutalities of totalitarian war. Men seem incapable of pursuing a good objective without creating new evils.

Vox populi vox dei is the greatest illusion in all political theory. The greater the number of people involved in Government, and the greater seem to be the ensuing evils. Tenney Frank, in his study of Roman Imperialism, has shown that it was when the whole citizen body of Rome began to exercise power that Rome embarked on a policy of imperialist expansion. The history of modern Europe most certainly demonstrates the same fact: the rise of empires kept pace with the extension of democracy.

Now, to conclude from all this that democracy is a political mistake would be a great error. That is the tragedy of the reactionary. Since man is dynamic, these changes from one social form to another are inevitable. We do not cure the evils of man by artificially seeking to preserve outworn institutions. On the contrary, we aggravate them. The seat of the evil lies deeper. Democracy, like every other political or social institution, merely reveals the corruption and contradiction that lies at the root of unredeemed human nature. "There is no health in us."

III

We have examined the workings of the law of corruption in history and in democracy as a specific phase of political development. Still more striking and disastrous is the operation of this law in the technological development of modern society.

Now by any and every common-sense standard, we would expect that improvement in the tools and machines of production would inevitably lead to much higher standards of living for everybody, and to greater social welfare. Increased power in the control of Nature would lead, so we should assume, to the greater happiness of the greater number. Precisely this was the expectation of the pioneer social philosophers of capitalism, and still more of the pioneers of Utopian socialism. What enchanting day-dreams they indulged in! What an idyllic prospect opens out for us, for example, in the pages of William Morris' *News from Nowhere*! There we see a world of upright, joyous, beautiful men and women; a society from which want and care have been banished; a community devoted to the pursuit of art and the cultivation of beauty. That was written eighty years ago. Can anyone, even the most purblind romantic, recognise any feature of Morris' utopia in the stark reality of contemporary society? Much truer to the actual situation and to its

emerging tendencies is the macabre horror of Mr.
Aldous Huxley's *Brave New World*, where men are
bred for purely subordinate functions. What has
happened is almost exactly the opposite of Morris'
rosy anticipations. "William Morris, in his *News from
Nowhere*, thought that the people in his utopia of the
future might read the novels of the nineteenth century
in order that the miseries recorded in them might
spice the happiness of their too perfect lives. Miseries
and troubles, indeed! If one turned to the closing days
of the nineteenth century now, it would be for another
reason—to recapture an incredible idyll of human
felicity." [1]

There is no need to waste time in showing how
technology has made of war a new evil. It has done so
in three directions. First, by intensifying a thousandfold
its powers of destruction; second, by making it
internally universal; third, by making it externally
universal. Let us briefly illustrate each of these.

There is no need to exaggerate the destructive
powers of contemporary science; for their actual scope
is terrible enough indeed. It took three months'
bombardment of Verdun in 1916, with millions of
heavy artillery shells, to reduce it to ruins. Twenty-six
years later I walked through the streets of Hull to
marvel at the ruination that five nights' blitzing with
thousands of bombs could effect. In another two years
the whole world was staggered at the capacity of a
single atomic bomb to wipe out an entire city. Today

[1] Lewis Mumford, *Faith for Living*, pp. 8-9. (Secker & Warburg, 1941).

we are told that a few hydrogen bombs fired thousands of miles away could devastate the United Kingdom.

Thus the distinction between the armed and unarmed has necessarily disappeared. I have already discussed the significance of this, which is my second point. And my third point follows. Localised war has become an anachronism. Scientific development in war has made it world-wide, and civilisation has now no refuge from barbarism. In the pre-scientific age, there were areas to which the barbarian could not penetrate, in which, therefore, culture and spiritual values could find shelter. Today, civilisation is breeding its own destructive barbarian from within and equips him with the technical apparatus to destroy his parent. The difference between the new barbarian which a secularised Europe has produced and the old barbarian of the so-called "Dark Ages" is that the new barbarian regards no refuge as sacred. In the disintegrating Empire of Rome, the Goth and the Hun restrained their lust to destroy when they encountered monastery or Church. The barbarian respected them. But not the new barbarian, whatever his guise. Modern technology has made us all potential barbarians.

But the evil created by the undoubted human good of scientific progress is by no means confined to war. In peace it has made possible a new degradation of humanity. We can study this aspect of it in the effects of industrialism upon slavery.[1]

Slavery is nearly as old as civilisation itself, but with

[1] Toynbee, op. cit., Vol. IV, pp. 137–41.

the breakdown of Roman civilisation, it became a declining institution in Western Europe. It is true, of course, that feudalism transformed it into serfdom, which was slavery at one remove. Whereas under chattel slavery—i.e. slavery proper—men and women were directly and wholly property, under serfdom they were indirectly owned by a system of land-tenure. But with the breakdown of feudalism, which began in the twelfth century, and with the rise of the towns, the serf developed into the freeman. Slavery ceased to be a dominating institution in Christendom and tended to relegate itself more and more to the colonial fringes. Even there it was dying a slow death. In the eighteenth century, slavery had passed away in the British colonies along the Atlantic seaboard as far north as the Mason-Dixon line, which Lincoln determined, at a later period, should be the limit of slavery in America. But how was it that an institution which had died a natural death in one Atlantic area, and was dying a slow death in other areas, suddenly acquired new life and vigour? The answer is to be found in the impact of industrialism, which was the offspring of science.

The increasing industralisation of Europe made heavy demands upon the supply of colonial raw materials, and especially food, to feed the machines and the urban proletariat respectively. Thus an old evil, which was in process of passing away, was galvanised into new life. And there began the horrors of the modern slave-trade than which there is nothing more appalling in the records of ancient slavery. African negroes were herded like cattle and transported, in conditions of indescribable cruelty, across the seas to North America. And it was in the most distinctively industrial activity of industrialism, namely cotton, that slavery experienced its greatest stimulus. In the Southern cotton-belt of the United States, which fed the textile industries of Lancashire with raw materials, slavery proved most resistant. Whereas slavery was abolished in British colonies in 1833 (except Hong Kong), it grew in the American South to monstrous proportions, until in 1861 it plunged America into the horrors of civil war. And that, even, was not the end of it.

Four years of civil war left behind a terrible legacy of hatred and bitterness, out of which has developed the dreadful racial problem of black and white—the outstanding shame of American politics and social life. *All this is in the trail of what is an undoubted human good.* Had slavery died a non-violent death in the American South, the probability is that America would have escaped its most intractable social problem, and its history would have been innocent of the lynchings, the inhuman segregations and other cruelties which now mar it. Technology, which is so instinct with magnificent possibilities of welfare, has here turned into an actuality of greed and bitterness and cruelty.

Without legally enslaving vast masses of people, both primitive and civilised, technology has made possible and actual an exploitation, which for savagery and consciencelessness, is not exceeded in the record of any legal slavery, ancient or modern. We have already made reference to the cruelties which in the early nineteenth century were inflicted upon *British* children in the textile industries. In the twentieth century, we had similar horrors imposed on Chinese children in the silk mills of Shanghai. But these horrors were, if possible, exceeded by the monstrosities of imperialism in its exploitation of the peoples of Africa and Asia, who were enslaved in all but name. And what are we to say to the economic and social improvement of the lot of the masses in Europe, when we remember that it was so largely based upon colonial exploitation? It rather takes the gilt off the ginger-bread, doesn't it! It was science—an unchallengeable human gain—that made the conditions of such exploitation possible.

And today, at the peak of technological development, this old evil of slavery enters on a new phase of horror and cruelty—and, if you please, in the service of scientific socialism, which is, historically, a progressive development of capitalism and imperialism. Technology is a pre-requisite of Marxian Socialism, out of which arises a new development of slavery!

The vast industrial machine of the modern world, with its theoretically unlimited horse-power, is the unique creation of science, in which the creative genius of man is supremely embodied. The private ownership and control of this machine has become socially impossible, hence the wars, civil wars and revolutions of our unhappy century. In the absence of a consciously-initiated alternative, history is forcing on the world a casual solution which has taken the form of the control of the entire economic and political apparatus by a single party which tolerates no opposition. That is, a group, a junta of men—for that is what dictator parties amount to—concentrate in their hands the whole power which science has created. Consequently and necessarily, freedom disappears. One cannot argue with men who contend that such a single-party constitution is the freest in the world. Such logic makes sense only in a madhouse. Russia, and, for a time, Germany arrived at the point maintained by ancient Egypt, though on a much higher plane, of course. The despots of Egypt had control of its entire wealth, and so made their subjects politically amenable by the simple device of starvation. By cutting off the supply of water to the canal system, the Egyptian tyrants effectively subdued rebellious provinces. Three thousand years of toil and tragedy brought parts of our world back to Egypt. By their control of the economic processes, made possible, let me repeat, by science, modern dictatorships reduced hundreds of millions of people to a new slavery. Compared with modern dictators, the ancient variety were mere tyros. To such a pass have we been brought by the blessings of technology, which rescues an old evil and invests it with new life and power.

But perhaps the greatest curse effected by science is that it fostered a mentality, an attitude of heart and soul, which makes any escape from the accumulating ills of our time increasingly difficult. There are two aspects of this fact to be considered.

The immense increase in productivity of the modern machine was made possible by an ever-wider extension of the principle of the subdivision of labour and standardisation of labour processes. Except for the tool-maker, and now the electronic machine controller, the vast majority of men employed in industry are engaged on single automatic processes. These masses of men (and women) spend their working day repeating the same process as the moving platform goes past them. They have ceased to be craftsmen and have become machine-minders. The skill is in the machine.

Now it is inevitable that such monotony and mechanical automatism is bound to affect the mind of the worker, especially over a long period. It has a deadening effect. It inhibits initiative and sense of individual responsibility. It stunts personality. And so there is bred in masses of men a mechanised mentality, which hands responsibility over to somebody else—the boss, the party, the dictator. They become, in Mr. Lewis Mumford's striking phrase, "passive barbarians". It is this passive barbarism which is the human root of dictatorship. "Thinking, direction, intelligence has concentrated itself more and more at the top, while the subordinate jobs, whether they are those of a book-keeper or an engineer or a salesman have become more impersonal, more mechanised, more irresponsible. This mechanisation, as long as it works, makes ordinary men carefree; that is, in return for their devotions, they have the reward that all slaves have—their masters can do the worrying. Here is the very medium for despotism to flourish in . . . Slavery at the bottom, caprice at the top; mechanisation at the bottom, raw savagery at the top; this is what society has come to." [1]

The active and passive barbarians are as closely related as the two sides of a penny. It is the passive barbarian, who exists in millions, even in countries with free traditions, that made the triumph of Nazism and Stalinism possible. In its hour of most dazzling achievements, Western science has fostered the growth of a mentality that helps to destroy civilisation. A very grim paradox indeed! It is these passive barbarians who looked on, fearing to *do* anything or say anything, during the years in which Hitler was clubbing Germany's finest elements to death.

Finally, science has strengthened enormously one of the most fatal of all the delusions of mortal man. It has deepened in the modern mind the assumption that it is possible to make *this* world yield complete security, and so turned men into the pursuit of the unrealisable.

The amazing conquests of science in the last hundred years have given rise, in the mind of today, to the illusion that, if only world peace could be secured, man's destiny is to be fulfilled in this world. If so much of Nature could be brought under human control, then surely much more could be conquered in time. Man's greatest need is not salvation but to be

[1] Lewis Mumford, *Faith for Living*, pp. 26-7 (Secker & Warburg, 1941).

freed from the menace of the nuclear bomb, when nothing could escape his almighty hand. Human destiny has come to be formulated in purely material terms. And in that spirit, culture and the things of the spirit have been materialised, deprived of their invisible, fourth dimension. Modern man has become wholly three-dimensional. The vision of sociology is that of an Age of Plenty, which, in turn, deepens the essential materialism of the age. Abundant consumption of material goods by everybody. With the realisation of that dream, man will at least reach the haven of complete security, when all demons and fears will be banished.

Now it is precisely this temper and anticipation that reduces our world to chaos. Thus technology is producing an attitude which endangers its own future development. The only thing that can preserve civilisation is the realisation by the common man that there are things of infinitely greater importance than maximum consumption of material goods, for the sake of which he must be prepared to sacrifice material wealth. But that violates the secularised mind of today. To continue with the idea that the destiny of man is to be realised fully in this world is to strengthen the spirit of materialism. If the spirit of materialism gets any stronger than it is now, it will mean the death of democracy and civilisation. Materialism makes passive barbarians, and passive barbarians make for the triumph of dictatorship. In the final analysis, technology, like democracy, produces its negating evil.

IV

Thus we can see the operation of a profound contradiction in the development of history, in the growth of political institutions, and in the evolution of man's technical power, the effect of which is that the good is neutralised and cursed by the evil to which it seems to give rise. It is like the old fable of the good and the bad fairies. The good fairies each endow the newborn child with a good gift. But the bad fairy comes along with her curse with the result that the good gifts produce only unhappiness. It was said of a famous statesman that he had all the gifts, except the gift to use them, which is a perfect parable of the impotence of mankind in history. "There is no health in us."

Now this contradiction, which we have observed in the social, institutional life of the race, is equally active in the personal life of individuals, to which fact modern psychology bears ample witness.

One of the most shattering revelations of psychoanalysis has been the denial that there exists a distinct class of abnormal people. In so-called normal people, abnormal tendencies are always operating in greater or less degree. Between normal and abnormal there is no distinct dividing line. Psycho-analysis has scientifically established that man is a sick soul, and often it shows that none are so sick as those who think themselves perfectly healthy. Jung coined the term "normal insanity" to express this fact. " 'Normal insanity' begins when the emotions are aroused. In these days

Down, Peacock's Feathers

we have ample opportunity to observe this process on a grand scale. We can see every form of mental contagion, from the crudest sentimentalism to the most subtle, secret poisoning of reason, *and this among the so-called normal people—the average individuals who largely make up a nation or state."* [1] The psychological study of suicide, particularly, of which there has been an alarming increase in recent decades, has thrown a flood of light upon the sickness of the average man.

We are all of us familiar with what William James called "the divided mind", the classical statement of which is to be found in Paul's epistle to the Romans.[2] This disintegration is the state of every human being. It is like a train with two engines, one pulling one way and the other pulling in the opposite way. This condition of the ego has been reformulated in modern psychology as the contradiction between the will-to-live and the will-to-die. Everybody is unconsciously motivated by a wish-to-die as well as by the urge to live.[3] The aspiration for life is turned into self-destructive channels.

It is not difficult to see this in the enormous increase of suicide in Europe and America in recent years. But the will-to-die operates, not only in direct attempts to kill oneself, but also in mass, institutional activities which circumscribe and reduce life, make it negative by suffering for suffering's sake. This was one of the

[1] *The Integration of the Personality*, p. 10 (Kegan Paul, Trench Trubner & Co., 1941). The italics are mine (D. R. D.).
[2] Chapter VII, verses 14–24.
[3] Freud, *Mourning and Melancholia*, in Collected Works (Hogarth Press).

psychological roots of Fascism, which became power-ful through the weakness of the masses. It is said that the *peoples* do not want war. No doubt it is true that *consciously* they do not want it. But unconsciously? Can it be seriously argued that wars would be so frequent, if people, deep down in their innermost being, did not want it?

Then there is the vast phenomenon with which we are all familiar of delight in being half dead. On this there is no need to enlarge. People don't feel healthy unless they are sick. Psychologists are mainly in agreement that this is the chief reason for chronic invalidism. We want to live *and die* at the same time.

The self-defeating character of human good is to be seen in all its bitterness in purely personal relationships, a tragic example of which is sex. How intermingled in sexual relationships are love and hate! However does it happen that two people who fall hopelessly in love with each other find their way to the divorce court? What dark tortuous thing is it that turns the exquisite ecstasy of love's young dream into the squalid boredom and monotony of marriage? There is a great deal of truth in the schoolboy's howler that "Christians are only allowed one wife and they call it holy monotony". [1] In the very best of marriages, the lines and tints of romance fade away into a commoner light. Why? To say that it is inevitable is no explanation

[1] Is not the correct version of this story: "A Mahommedan may have many wives—this is called polygamy. A Christian may have only one wife—this is called monotony"?

of it. Like everything else human ecstasy is self-destructive.

But the negation of good in personal relationships is seen more clearly in the process of rationalisation and self-deception, which, again, is illumined for us in modern psychology.

Complete disinterestedness of behaviour and attitude is, in fact, never achieved in human experience. In every good action or thought or concern, some element of self-will is intruded. The New Testament expresses this fact by saying that "we love God because He first loved us". In all human goodness, there is something of selfish gain and interest, and this self-seeking motive often neutralises the good that we do. Man is incapable of a goodness completely objective. We do good partly because we thereby benefit ourselves. One of the conditions for doing a good act—i.e. some act of service, of altruistic intent—is that, consciously or (more frequently) unconsciously, such an act shall satisfy our will-to-power. And individual will-to-power is the root of sin.

Now in the individual, this process is very involved, obscure and disguised. But we get a very obvious example in the behaviour of nations, one in which the process is seen in the raw, without any disguise. No nation ever acts with complete disinterestedness. Nations will serve and promote social good only when such good coincides with the interests of its own power-politics. Britain, for example, fights for the ideal of freedom and the security of civilisation only when her own existence and national position are endangered. Only when the two interests have combined. Not to see this is either hypocrisy or sheer self-deception. Everything that is meant by European civilisation was directly menaced the moment Hitler came to power in 1933. His internal atrocities on Jews, Socialists, Marxists, Liberals and Christians failed to stir Britain to action. His external aggression was not resisted until it reached the point of danger to our survival and interests. The same thing is true of America, which becomes an active champion of democracy only when it is clear that America itself is directly menaced: when the uncovenanted mercy of the Atlantic Ocean ceases to be effective.

Now this process which, in the behaviour of nations, is so direct and on the surface, is, in individuals, indirect, hidden and camouflaged. That is to say, *it is rationalised*. Conduct which is, in part, self-regarding in motive is thought of by the individual concerned as altruistic and unselfish. The self-will is disguised. We refuse to admit to ourselves its activity. Thus individual conduct is a vast mechanism of self-deception. Men never face the naked truth. Direct accusation always calls forth a defence mechanism. With the best will in the world, we resent any attempt which seeks to destroy the picture we entertain of our own motives and character.

Obvious examples are provided in the relations of husband and wife and parent and child. The family is still the sphere of greatest tyranny in society. A man may love his wife sincerely, and a woman her husband. And such love may be, in part, genuinely objective and disinterested. But mixed up in it is individual will-to-power and self-seeking, the proof of which is reaction to criticism. Love is at its most ecstatic when mutual acceptance is most uncritical. How many husbands can listen to criticism from their wives without resentment? and how many wives from their husbands? But if love is wholly other and objective, why should one bristle and fume at criticism? The supreme difficulty and discipline of marriage lies precisely in the fact that it is the relation in which two egotisms are most intimately connected. Love seeks to translate itself into absolute possession, which every ego resents. Good is achieved only by conflict.

The lust for domination displays itself no less in the relation of a parent to child. The love which is borne by a parent for child is probably the deepest, the most passionate, and the most nearly disinterested in the world. We will do for our children what we will not do so willingly and spontaneously for anybody else. But the very intensity of that love carries with it an equally fierce possessiveness. When a child is most helpless and dependent then tenderness towards it is at its maximum. The complete dependence of another human being upon me is a profound satisfaction of my ego. But when a child has grown sufficiently to assert its will *against* me, something other than tenderness creeps into my feelings. We disguise from ourselves the real nature of our reactions. Our anger, our domination, our suppressions become concern for the welfare of our children. Our sole concern, we say to ourselves, is the good of the child. But far down in our irrational depths, it is the impudent challenge to our will-to-power that obsesses us.

This mechanism of self-deception operates (to use the language of the psychologists) through *displacement* and *projection*. The emotions which are centred upon a direct object are diverted to an indirect object. The feelings of hatred or anger, for instance, felt by an individual towards some frustrating authority, like a father or teacher, are diverted on to a group or institution. To a Nazi, the Jews constituted such an indirect object; to a Communist, the capitalist class or the bourgeoisie. And behind that disguise, the individual vents the hatred and bitterness which he dare not admit to himself.

Projection is more complicated. It consists in thinking that other people are like our own unrecognised and unadmitted selves. We endow others with the character which we will not admit to be true to ourselves. We attribute to others, for example, meanness of motive without any evidence. That, as we say, is our "impression", our "intuition". This is probably the motive behind political and religious persecution. It is more comfortable to hate what we feel to be wrong in others than to hate it in ourselves. In order to bypass self-accusation, the individual will project on others the moral judgment and condemnation of his own heart. This is particularly true of revolutionists, who nearly always exaggerate the evil of what they are fighting against, and then when they get power, proceed to commit the same evil on a bigger scale. And they do it with a greater ruthlessness, with a calculated cruelty. Displacement and projection enable the individual to make a peaceful companion of guilt and self-judgment.

Self-negation of our own good is thus a permanent activity in history and personal experience. We can see it at work in the historic process of the rise and fall of successive civilisations, bringing every one of them to destruction. We can see it in the development of democracy, thus mocking the hopes and dreams of its founders and pioneers. We witness it too in the amazing story of the triumphs of technology. And we see its baleful effects in the intimate sphere of individual personality. What conclusion can we draw from all this except the profound affirmation of the General Confession, that "there is no health in us"?

So whatever else in the Confession may be ghostly or abstract or remote, this dogma of the universal sickness of man is concrete and material enough. It is the very stuff of history and politics and economics and science and psychology. Man is incurably self-destructive. In this matter, it is the secular sociologies which have been proved to be fantastic, remote and delusive, and the General Confession to be sober, relevant and realist. The final, tragic truth about man in history is that there is no health in him.

Five

THE FRUITS OF REPENTANCE

"But Thou, O Lord, have mercy upon us, miserable
offenders. Spare Thou them, O God, which confess
their faults. Restore Thou them that are penitent.

NOTHING HAS BEEN A SUBJECT FOR GREATER
merriment or jeering raillery in the pages of our modern novelists than that part of the Confession in which
people describe themselves as "miserable offenders". I
seem to remember that H. G. Wells found this a particularly rich vein for his brilliant and riotous pen.
With incomparable facility for skinning people's souls,
he pictured Anglican congregations which, of course,
were very bourgeois, very complacent and very respectable, describing themselves, with the greatest
hypocritical gusto, as "miserable offenders". And
somehow the whole Confession withered away in the
contempt that flowed from Wells' pen. And how his
readers—of whom I was one—rocked with laughter.
That is a long time ago, and today we are rocking with
something that is very different from laughter. Before
he died, Wells himself had ceased to laugh.[1]

We are still a long way from the realisation that we
are "offenders" or sinners. "Sin" has not, even yet,

[1] *The Fate of Homo Sapiens*, pp. 106-7 (Secker & Warburg, 1939).

achieved the distinction of ranking as a serious sociological idea. There may be a growing conviction that,
in the modern world, men have been mistaken, or
foolish or superficial—that is to say, that in some way
or other they have been deficient. But to no appreciable
extent is there any widespread feeling that men are
guilty of sin, that they are "offenders" against a Holy
God. Defective, yes, but sinful, no. There is certainly
a growing suspicion that there is something wrong
somewhere. Perhaps our formulas have been erroneous. Our principles, possibly, have been inadequate.
Our policies have certainly proved unavailing. There is
much in the superstructure of social life that is mistaken. But of a realisation that what is wrong is the
very heart and core, the deep foundations of history,
there is very little trace. The very physical impacts of
our time have compelled some sort of intellectual
revisions, but not a spiritual overturn.

One of the lazy and very dangerous assumptions of
men in all ages, including our own, is that disaster
automatically leads to repentance. The modern gospel
of progress, by emptying repentance of its element of
tragic despair, considerably strengthened the expectation that all the good things happen automatically. But
they do not. On the contrary, very much on the contrary. As G. K. Chesterton used to say: "If you want to
keep a white post white, you must continually repaint
it white. Leave it alone, and it will get black." But
somehow or other, we have assumed that change,
reform, amelioration, is a necessary by-product of

suffering and failure. Marx was cocksure that revolutionary consciousness in the workers was a necessary consequence of capitalist development.[1] History has belied him. It was Lenin who corrected Marx on this point by showing that capitalist development merely creates discontent, which, if it is to become revolutionary, must be transformed by ideas brought to the workers by intellectual revolutionaries.[2] It was thought that the experience of world war would inevitably lead to world peace. "Never again," said Lloyd George as he saw the remarkable vision of a new Jerusalem rising up out of Hell. But the disaster of the First World War led, by convulsive zigzags, to the still greater disaster of a second, which everyone saw to be a continuation of the first.

In purely personal, individual life, disaster does not produce repentance any more than it does in social life, when one would expect it to do so. Disaster in marriage does not, automatically, induce in men and women the humble acknowledgment of their respective responsibility—that is, repentance. What is automatic about it is the divorce-court and a new disaster. Some Hollywood actors, for instance, change their wives as often as some men change their shirts. Henry VIII has long since lost his record. The rarest thing in personal moral failure is the realisation of one's own responsibility. It is nearly always circumstances, or somebody else. Hardly ever oneself.

[1] *Capital*, Vol. I, pp. 836-7. (Kerr & Co., Chicago).
[2] *What is to be Done?*, pp. 32-3 (Lawrence & Wishart).

So the supreme disaster of European civilisation in our day does not bring repentance. Men do not cry in increasing numbers—"*peccavi*" (I have sinned). The General Confession, when it says that we are "miserable offenders", therefore, is still awaiting serious recognition. But in one thing, at least, we have caught up with the General Confession. We are certainly "miserable", even if we refuse to acknowledge that we are "miserable offenders". Throughout the Western world today there is nothing more certain than the unhappy state of the hearts of men and women. Fear of the future possesses parents who dread what lies in store for their children, and the children born in an atmosphere of fear see destruction awaiting them. We were unhappy during the war, but that unhappiness is nothing compared with what afflicts us in this nuclear age of spiritual isolation and terror. "We are miserable . . ."

Our leaders in political and social life do not doubt, of course, what needs to be done, if mankind is to continue its progress through the Welfare State to Utopia. In an output of books without precedent in this country and the United States, which started after the war and continues unabated, writers have been telling us what we have got to do to be (perhaps) saved. One of the most striking things in my recent experience as a parish priest, in which I talk to numbers of ordinary people, who are not intellectuals either of the Right or the Left or of any other position of geographical location, is that I very seldom hear confident assertions that we as a nation know where we are going. In a very dim, cloudy sort of way, they seem to sense some deep unplumbed dimension in this business of threatening war and possible peace and a new social order. But whatever our judgment of it may be, the fact remains that while there is wistful hope, there is no equal certainty to match it. It is a situation in which nearly all the elements of repentance are present—nearly all. Yet there is no tide or torrent of repentance. There is no noticeable crying out: "Spare Thou them, O God, which confess their faults . . . have mercy upon us, miserable offenders." In mediaeval Europe, during the calamity of the Black Death, the masses flocked to Church to pray for mercy. They felt that the plague was a divine judgment. But today the masses do not flock anywhere. Except to football matches and the TV screen. And they do not pray for mercy. And divine judgment has become an alien, unfamiliar idea. *And we are impotent.* Is there no organic connection here, between this inner unawareness of judgment and the outer confusion and paralysis?

I

The first element in repentance is the realisation of personal individual responsibility and guilt before God. It is the point at which a man will say to himself: "The blame for my failure and my wrong-doing is *mine*; *I* have disobeyed God." It is a consciousness of personal responsibility to God. Without the feeling that it is

137

God who has been disobeyed, there can be no *repentance*. Responsibility obtains only in a personal relationship. One can feel responsibility about society, for example, only if one realises society as somehow personal, as a personal reality transcending itself. To society as an abstraction or an impersonal institution one may feel legal obligation, which is far removed from moral responsibility. It is a very common fact that people will do things in relation to institutions, without compunction, which, if they did them to persons, would make them feel guilty. A man who would not dream, for example, of stealing from individuals will cheerfully rob or cheat a railway company, or the State. As he puts it, they are fair game. The tax-payer operates with a different conscience from that which censors him in his personal dealings. Even in the best of men, conscience speaks less sharply in institutional relations than it does in personal relations. Responsibility is an affair of persons.

This muffling of conscience in relation to institutional behaviour is part of a much wider phenomenon in our time, which is profoundly symbolical. We have lived to witness the emergence of a disastrous contradiction in the relations of society and the individual, which is acutely relevant to the question of repentance. In the last hundred years, we have seen the rise of what has come to be called "the social conscience", which has proved to be, in practice, a twisted, distorted reflection of the Christian ideal of human brotherhood. It was a process by which the warm, living and tender concern for men as persons, sons of a common Father, was transformed into a remote, abstract, institutional feeling of obligation. In Marxist Communism men became masses. This feeling was a compound mixture of contradictory elements. It was partly fear, largely egoistic class interest. This huge proletarian beast, crouching in its foetid lair, would spring one fine day, if he were not better fed. The propaganda of the First International created and fomented this fear. The *Communist Manifesto's* "a spectre is haunting Europe", really did frighten the middle classes in the latter half of last century, as was proved by the cruel excesses of the French bourgeoisie against the Paris Commune. Fat little Thiers was the predecessor of the long and lean Pétain, the difference between whom significantly symbolises the degeneration of society between 1870 and 1940. It was partly an expression of bourgeois snobbishness, which found a good deal of exercise in the Socialist Movement. Trotsky points this out in his criticism of Ramsay MacDonald, who once wrote: "In the realm of feeling and conscience, in the realm of spirit, Socialism forms the religion of service to the people." "In those words," remarks Trotsky, "is immediately betrayed the benevolent bourgeois, the left Liberal, who 'serves' the people, coming to them from one side or more truly from above." [1] This feeling of obligation was partly, also a reflection of a genuine objective concern and sympathy for the oppressed and

[1] Trotsky's *Where is Britain Going?*, p. 53 (Communist Party of Great Britain, 1926).

exploited, though even in that there was deep, obscure egoism. But the point which should be clearly grasped is that the social conscience which has characterised a secularised, capitalist society *in decline* was a concern for men in the mass rather than as personal individuals.

By the 'seventies of the nineteenth century, the conception of society as a self-existent entity had become dominant. It was the final logic of a long process, stretching back to the Renaissance. The break-up of mediaeval Christendom as a single society deriving its life from God led to the idea of society, within the framework of the absolute, sovereign state, as deriving its life from itself. The sense of God as a present, living Reality in men's lives had grown dim. Hence the feeling that men were sons of God, and, therefore, brothers, was transmuted into the idea that they were masses, whose conditions must be improved. Improve the conditions and you improve their souls—a colossal miscalculation (which does *not* mean that Christianity is indifferent to conditions). In Seebohm Rowntree's last survey of York, there was evidence for the statement that to improve conditions was considered equivalent to improving souls—evidence also for the fallacy of it.[1] Physical conditions had greatly improved in York since 1901. More parks, better houses, better food, etc., but more vacant minds, mass-produced ideas, tastes, and so on. God, the Almighty Father, had ceased to be a reality in the minds of the vast majority

[1] *Poverty and Progress*, Part III, pp. 329–477 (Longmans, 1941).

of men. They had lost emotional content, living awareness. Inevitably, men ceased to be personal in their responsibility and regard for one another.

In the end, this came to mean not only in York but everywhere that improvement was a job for somebody else—societies, movements, the state—but not for one-self. The social conscience hardened into institutionalism. We are our brother's keeper, certainly. But we will organise it, delegate it, mechanise it. Which is what happened. It was no accident that Neville Chamberlain should ask, over the wireless, in September, 1938, that appalling question: "Why should we fight for a country (Czechoslovakia) so far away?" [1] That was the quintessence of the heart and mind of an entire era. To blame Chamberlain only was cowardly humbug. He spoke for a generation to whom God as Father, had become meaningless. If God is my Father, then men are my brothers, whether they be Nazis or Marxists. We might sum up our time as a period in which men felt, not individual personal responsibility for their fellows, but a delegated institutional obligation. Communists themselves, alive to the needs of fellow-communists in Europe, were less sensitive to the terrors inflicted on opponents of Marxism. Catholics, ablaze against the persecution of priests in Republican Spain, were indifferent to the Franco murder of Basque priests who happened to support the Republic. All this expressed, not personal responsibility, but

[1] It is surely only fair to add that Chamberlain went on to explain that much more was at stake than this?

awakened egoism, as distinct from blind and somnolent egoism. Social conscience emptied of personal responsibility.

Now, the recovery of personal responsibility, even as a social factor, depends upon the realisation by men of their responsibility to God, upon Whom and from Whose will society depends and derives. *And responsibility is tied up with the awakening of the sense of sin.* Let the reader not delude himself on this point. "Have mercy upon us, miserable offenders." We all have to come to the point of saying to ourselves: "Thou art the man". We have to reverse the natural tendency by which we excuse ourselves as "more sinned against than sinning", and realise, with depth and intensity, that we have sinned against far more than we have been sinned against. The wrongs we may have suffered at the hands of society and our fellows are but as a drop in the ocean compared to the wrongs we have committed against God. Now to see ourselves in this position until it hurts is the first step in repentance. To strike a just balance in the apportioning of blame between human beings for wrongs done and suffered is impossible. It is forever beyond the wit and power of man. But nothing is easier than to do so in the relations between God and man; for all the wrong done is on one side, and all the wrong suffered is on the other. Therefore let men look to themselves for the culprit. "For we have all sinned and fallen short of the glory of God." For each one to cry out: "Have mercy upon us, miserable offenders. Spare thou them, O God, *which confess their faults*"—that will do more for the cleansing and renewal of our world than all the new social programmes put together. In short repentance.

It is infinitely difficult! For man to abandon radically his pride of self-will; to relinquish his *hubris*—what St. John calls "pride of life"—is more difficult than initiating revolutions and fundamental social change, which, for all their tragedy, are but dynamic transformations of the forms in which pride expresses itself. Even when faced by the ruin and collapse of our way of life, repentance is still difficult. The unreality of God to man makes repentance impossible. Of the two fundamental elements of repentance—realisation of God as real (whatever be the degree of such realisation) and final conviction of the evil of self-will—the basic conditions for the latter certainly obtain in our present situation.

Man must have bitter experience and certain proof of the futility of his self-will before he can come to despair of himself, which is what conviction of the disaster of self-will induces. History speaks with one voice on this fact. If civilisations were continually progressive and never bred contradictions, human pride would be unchallengeable. As we used to say about the Germans, defeat is necessary for them to undergo change of heart. What we forget is that what was true of Germans in the military sphere is even more true of man as man in the spiritual sphere. Germans share in common human nature. By the accident of history, that particular characteristic of human nature happened to function more obviously in a military fashion with them. But men everywhere, and at all times, whatever their race or class, will not question their pride so long as they are making a success of it. On a diet of continuous victories, pride is unconquerable. Defeat of self-will is a necessary preliminary for repentance. It does not necessarily ensue even then. Without it, it certainly will not.

It is surely obvious that that condition is more than realised today so long after the war. Everybody agrees that from the moment of victory things have gone hopelessly wrong. Nobody claims that our civilisation and way of life are so fine that they ought to be continued unchanged. We are all agreed on the fact of failure, however we differ about the causes of the failure. But even so there is no turning away from self, no despair of self. Indeed, the whole problem is so vast, that what is really happening is that men and women are refusing to face it, and are trying to shelter themselves in an acquiescence in a fate *which will demand nothing of them*. To come to the God of Jesus Christ in repentance challenges pride. To submit to a fate of some kind makes no such radical demand.

Resort to astrology has increased greatly in recent years, especially since the war. Adherents of this new religion are to be found amongst every class, among them well-educated people and many professing Christians. Significantly enough, not among Roman Catholics. The Church which has refused to make any doctrinal compromise with modern thought provides fewest recruits for the revival of Babylonian and Chaldean mysteries.

What is the effect of all this? It is manifold. It intensifies the reluctance to admit responsibility. More serious, however, if possible, is the intensification of sheer irrationalism and delusion. The principle operative factor is the moment of birth, and success depends upon being born at the right moment: failure, upon the same cause. But as the astrological method is so obscure it is almost always possible to arrive at an optimistic forecast. The immediate effect is therefore usually favourable to fantasy, and fatally disposes one to concentrate upon one's personal interests. Women especially are tempted to this form of self-deception, and to seeking for guidance that suits their own dispositions. Just as a drug-addict resorts to dope when oppressed by a consciousness of impotence, so these addicts to astrology turn in increasing numbers to spiritual drugs when oppressed by the realisation that any situation is completely beyond them. Spiritual helplessness, which could be the first step to repentance, becomes a deeper descent into the abyss of self-will. More than ever does our contemporary world emphasise the relevance of the General Confession to the historic predicament of man.

II

The result, or fruit, of repentance is the realisation of a new relation to God. "Restore Thou them that are penitent." First, the confession of faults—that is, recognition of responsibility before God; then restoration. What does this mean?

One of the many obstacles to the enjoyment of Christian experience and Christian understanding by our generation is the survival of a crude and false anthropomorphism. It has become a settled idea in the mind of our time, when it thinks at all about Christian truth, that God seems to be actuated by the petty and mean motives which men experience. This is a survival of Protestant Scholasticism. To a mind which is at home only on the surface of theological problems, there seems much to justify this attitude. God, for example, is "a jealous God". Straight away, we think of jealousy where it is most prevalent in human experience—in sexual relations. So that's what God is like! Men congratulate themselves that they need not trouble to come to terms with such a God. "For if ye forgive not men their trespasses, neither will God forgive your trespasses." Did Jesus really say that? Tit-for-tat apparently! So here it seems that God is insisting on His dignity. Unless you own up to your faults, God won't play, so to speak.

A little depth of thinking should make apparent that there's something wrong in thinking of God in this crude way. The God and Father of the Lord Jesus Christ, at least, is not an enlarged egoist. It is profoundly true that without repentance there is no restoration, not because God spitefully refuses, but because only repentance can create in men the desire and capacity for the new relation which God Himself has made possible. Repentance is to stop doing what you are doing and to say "No" to yourself. Before you attempt to do anything, you own up and wait. At that moment God acts. "Spare, Thou, them that confess their faults . . . Restore, Thou, them that are penitent." Confession is the essential preliminary to restoration. This is not quixotry, but a profound moral necessity.

Natural law offers an analogy. Law secures service and effectiveness, if it is obeyed, if men hold the right attitude to it. By adapting or subordinating their desires to conformity with law in nature, nature becomes benevolent to human welfare. But disobedience to natural law entails destructive consequences. Any attempt to subordinate fixed law to varying desire makes nature malevolent. That is the fundamental condition of existence.

So it is in the realm of spirit. Caprice is not a feature of spiritual being. Only like can understand like. Only deep calleth unto deep. An unwillingness to forgive, for example, means that a man cannot feel the need or desire for forgiveness. The forgiving temper creates the humble longing to be forgiven. Without the sense of need for forgiveness we remain blind to the fact that God has already forgiven us, which means that divine forgiveness cannot be appropriated. So with repentance. To realise that one is out of accord with God is the first step towards getting into accord with Him. Having confessed one's state of sin, restoration follows, because realisation of the need for it has come into the heart.

The reader will recall, at this point, that, according to the Biblical revelation, man's state in time is not the original state in which God created him. History is not a reflection of the original relation in which man stood to his Creator. History is a record of distortion, indeed a perversion of what man was at his creation. By self-willed rebellion against God, man has converted the love of God into its opposite, and made it wrath, just as by disobedience to law man compels nature to become a destructive force. Egocentricity falsifies God's intention. The supreme need of man in his earthly life is to restore the original relation to God; to recreate the state in which God first created him. In terms of theology, the great problem is to repair the defaced image of God in man. In terms of sociology, how to create a new source and ground of human behaviour; how to fashion a determining will other than that of self-will? The basic, natural instinct of man is self-affirmation. Without thinking, we instinctively regard everything in the light of self-interest, and deliberate, rational thought is very largely a deceptive rationalisation of our deepest self-interest. How can we *naturally*, basically, come to regard everything first of all and all the time in the light of the interest of others? How can mankind invest altruism with as powerful an instinctive urge and vitality as now possesses egoism? That is the decisive, cardinal issue in historic development.

To the solution of that issue the General Confession

points the way. "Restore, Thou, them that are penitent" means to initiate the process by which altruism displaces egoism as the fundamental urge of men and women. This is the potential restoration of man to the state he was in before the Fall, which subsequent experience makes increasingly actual. This is the restoration of the marred image of God to its original purity. By repentance, life becomes the means for subordinating self to God, and not merely a means, as hitherto, for finding new historic expression for self-will. It is the beginning of the Great Retreat of Satan in personal and social life. Whereas before repentance, egocentricity is waging an apparently successful offensive war, after repentance it beats a retreat, entering upon a defensive war. There may be local sallies and counter-attacks of the old man, but the character of the campaign, as a whole, has undergone a drastic revolutionary change, for the new man has emerged.

How does this work in actual experience? What is the practical reality of this life of repentance as distinct from all humbugging pretence and self-deceiving rationalisation? What radical difference does it make in the life of him who has undergone the change? And what is its significance for political and social life? Very important questions!

To begin on a plane of realistic acknowledgment, we must dismiss, once and for all, any illusion that repentance initiates a process of perfection; that becoming a Christian means that sin ceases. This illusion is the counterpart in orthodox Christianity of the secular illusion of Utopia and the perfectibility of human nature. Here in time and flesh, Christians, however saintly they may become—and very few Christians become saints—never escape completely the inward contamination of original sin. Christians remain sinners, though a different sort of sinner—assuming that their Christianity is genuine, which is not a matter for human judgment. This is, of course, an occasion for humiliation. But it is a fact, and we must come to terms with it. So long as we feel an instinctive urge to self-will, we are still guilty of sin before God. And even should we cease to be conscious of such an urge, we still are sinners. Indeed, very dangerous sinners. Christians who have ceased to be aware of the operations of the old Adam are in a perilous condition. They are dangerously near the delusive state of assuming that the Holy Ghost is always in perfect agreement with them. And that is the very devil! The deeper a man's Christianity becomes, the more acute does his consciousness of sin become. For, however deep, obscure and subtle are the operations of self-will, they do not escape the penetrating light of awakened self-awareness. At the highest peaks of Christian achievement, the deep, dark unconscious has been brought into consciousness, almost entirely. Very little of the abysmal being remains in shadow, beyond the rays of central awareness. When Grace has been at work, very few doors remain locked; Satan wears no disguise which the eye of faith cannot penetrate. This is the peak of Christian triumph in the flesh. But if sin is present on the summit, how much more so on the lower slopes. The great souls at the top have no illusions. It is the fussy darlings lower down that suffer self-intoxication. It is often clear in the valley when there is a mist on the mountain-top.

It is failure to realise that this must be so that is the source of so much of the censure which the non-Christian passes on the Churches. God knows the Churches are miserable enough specimens of Christian life and thought. But the criticisms of the world reveal at least as much shallow self-righteousness and deluded unawareness of self as that of even the most imperfect Christian. Take, for example, the strictures which the Left delivers against the Church. They never betray a hint that the critics themselves are ever assailed by doubts of their own disinterestedness and righteousness. Oh no! They are prophetic souls. Like Elijah, they are oppressed by the spectacle (which certainly needs no magnifying glass) of these people, calling themselves Christian, who bow down so low before the Baal of Capitalism, and the disguisements of brutalised power, that it becomes a moral duty and an act of holy indignation to kick their conveniently elevated posteriors. And with what ecstasy do they perform that particular duty! What a kick they receive out of the kick which they give, thus proving that "it is more blessed to receive than to give". But how much of their blistering vision of the iniquities of the Church is itself the expression of their own egocentricity? They show little sign of being aware of such a disturbing possibility—a possibility revealed, not by theology, but by psycho-analysis. There is little accent of charity in their tumultuous tirades; little sense of being fellow-travellers in sin and suffering. So cocksure of Christianity are those who never worship with fellow-sinners or partake of the mystery of the Body and the Blood—that they have no ear for what the Church has to say except when what the Church says echoes themselves. They cannot conceive that there is any sincerity or reality in the Church's fear of the atheism of the socialist movement, especially on the Continent, and of its deadly danger for the future of mankind. Charlie Marx has settled that question for them. And this is only one example.

To expect Christians to act consistently by the standard of the Sermon on the Mount, betrays a serious failure to understand the sociology of sin, and a still more serious spirit of nauseating self-righteousness, which Christ regarded as the supreme sin. The Christian does not emerge full-grown out of the bitter waters of repentance. He arises from that grim depth a chastened and humiliated man.

There is, of course, a danger in this realisation of the historic impossibility of Christian consistency, namely, the conclusion that conduct is unimportant—which would be a calamitous error. Here, as in the whole range of Christian thought and action, Christian experience is a tension of opposites. We have to learn, on the one hand, that to perform consistently the Christian ethic is an impossibility. On the other hand, Christians have to proceed as though it were possible, and that every failure should be an occasion for penitence and renewed conviction of sin. These certainly are contradictions, but contradictions which indubitably exist as realities in every Christian experience. This is the "Yea" and the "Nay" of Christian ethical behaviour.

What then are the fruits of repentance?

They are all implied in that pearl of great price, Humility. Humility is the germ-seed which grows into the Tree of Life, on which every Christian virtue will flower, and the leaves of which will be "for the healing of the nations". Humility is a *fruit*, an immediate fruit, of repentance. It is a spontaneous happening, something which the truly penitent suddenly discovers within himself. It is not a deliberately-willed duty, a painfully-pursued objective. It is miraculously, unaccountably there, the source of the deepest joy in Christian experience, the realisation that one is dependent on Another for every good in one's being. This is the new creation in Christ.

> *O Jesus Christ, grow Thou in me,*
> *Let all things else recede.*

Humility makes possible the growth of a new will, which springs out of God. It is this new will which initiates in men the process of making altruism natural, just as egoism is natural in the old will. Humility is the only true and abiding revolution in human relationships, the only revolution whose work has not to be done over again. Out of it come all the virtues of the

Christian life, which St. Paul has enumerated in a classic passage. "The fruit of the Spirit, is love, joy, peace, long-suffering, gentleness, goodness, faith, meekness, temperance . . ."

The significance of Humility in social relationships is beyond reckoning. It will be enough if I indicate it in one direction only—our present international situation.

In politics, self-righteousness is a fruitful source of cruelty, stupidity and hatred. The consciousness that we are altogether in the right, and that our enemies and opponents are altogether in the wrong diverts and perverts the energies of conscience to the pursuit of evil policies, which, in good time, compel men to reap the whirlwind of conflict. One example of self-righteousness which has trailed the footsteps of European history since the First World War, was the guilt-clause of the Versailles Peace Treaty, which compelled the Germans to acknowledge that theirs was the entire guilt of the war. It was the Allies' great sin. What a different Europe should we have seen had the statesmen and diplomats who had gathered in the grandeur of Versailles to make peace been conscious that none were guiltless, that before God all were sinners.

Today, the same claim to absolute sovereignty is made by all nations, for absolute sovereignty is nothing less than national determination to persist in the righteousness of its own will, with the result that the United Nations is desperately weakened, and power blocks face each other in terrible earnest, each relying upon its own right, each certain of its own cause, each rebelling against God in its own egotism, each setting up itself as its own centre.

The destinies of the world in the immediate future depend upon the realisation by statesmen that they, and the peoples they represent, are all sinners. There can be no reasonable doubt that history will apportion the major responsibility for the catastrophe of the last war at the door of the Nazis. That is certain. But no nation will be entirely free. That is equally certain. We *may* save the rising generation of the peoples of the world incalculable tragedy and suffering if, even now in the midst of the strains and tension of human political relations, and the grotesque threats of nuclear destruction on the one hand, or totalitarian world slavery on the other, we resist the asphyxiating fumes of self-interest, remembering that we are all bound together in a community of calamity and sin. But such a realisation demands individual and national Humility, and Humility is a fruit of repentance. So we had better pay heed to the General Confession: "Have mercy upon us, miserable Offenders." All of us.

Six

CHRIST'S REVELATION OF
THE MEANING OF HISTORY

*". . . according to Thy promises declared unto mankind
in Christ Jesus, our Lord."*

THE RESTORATION OF MAN TO HIS FULL ORIGINAL
relation to God is the supreme purpose of history. It is
its *raison d'être*. This is Christ's revelation. "According to
Thy promises declared unto mankind in Christ Jesus,
our Lord", is in essence, in very concentrated essence,
the Christian philosophy of history. To bring men and
women into repentance, to initiate them into a new
life, to start them on a new career in which love displaces egoism, is the end to which history is working.
This is what Christ means for history, and what history
means for the Christian. The ultimately significant act
in history is the repentance of individual men and
women. That is why "There is more joy in heaven
over one sinner that repenteth than over ninety-nine
just men." The things that impress the world, the great
events, the movements, the cataclysms, the revolutions,
the pomps and panoplies, are important only in their
relation to the experience of personal repentance.
Nothing of this ever strikes the headlines. But it is the
thing that supremely matters. When John Smith, one

of the world's "great unknown", repents in dust and ashes, more has been done for the world, for historic development, than when Summit Conferences are held. At long last, we should understand that the world's great events find meaning simply in the spiritual revolution in John Smith's heart and soul. This is the implication and the logic of the promise which God has made to man in the incarnation of our Lord Jesus Christ. "But now once for all at the consummation of the ages, He has been manifested to put away sin through His sacrifice" (Hebrews ix. 26).

I

In his Burge Memorial Lecture, *Christianity and Civilisation*[1] Dr. Arnold Toynbee asserted this as the meaning of history, in his own learned and illuminating manner. His statement is of such great importance that it deserves extended description and quotation.

There are, says Dr. Toynbee, three possible views of the relations between civilisation and Christianity. The first is that Christianity is the enemy of civilisation, which was that of Marcus Aurelius, the Emperor Julian and of the English historian, Gibbon. In the destruction of the Graeco-Roman world, Gibbon attributed as much influence to Christianity as to Barbarism: "I have described the triumph of barbarism and religion." The second view is that Christianity is the handmaid, the servant of civilisation. Christianity is a

[1] Published by the Student Christian Movement, 1940.

transitional thing which bridges the gap between one civilisation and another, "and", says Dr. Toynbee, "I confess that I myself held this rather patronising view for many years. On this view you look at the historical function of the Christian Church in terms of the process of the reproduction of civilisations. Civilisation is a species of being which seeks to reproduce itself, and Christianity has had a useful but a subordinate role in bringing two new secular civilisations to birth after the death of their predecessor." [1] The real significance of Christianity, on this view, and the service it renders to history is that it stimulates the growth of civilisation, that, for instance, it fostered the growth of modern European capitalist civilisation. This view may appeal to the dwindling numbers of those who unreservedly admire our civilisation, hardly to anybody else.

The third view is that civilisations, in their prosperity and decay, exist *to facilitate the development of Christianity in the world.* "The breakdowns and disintegrations of civilisations might be stepping-stones to higher things on the religious plane. After all, one of the deepest spiritual laws that we know is the law that is proclaimed by Aeschylus in the two words πχθει μχθος—'it is through suffering that learning comes'—and in the New Testament in the verse 'whom the Lord loveth, He chasteneth; and scourgeth every son whom He receiveth'. If you apply that to the rise of the higher religions which has culminated in the flowering of Christianity, you might say that in the mythical pas-

---

[1] *Christianity and Civilisation*, p. 15.

sions of Tammuz and Adonis and Attis and Osiris, the Passion of Christ was foreshadowed, and that the Passion of Christ was the culminating and crowning experience of the sufferings of human souls in successive failures in the enterprise of secular civilisation. The Christian Church itself arose out of the spiritual travail which was a consequence of the breakdown of the Graeco-Roman civilisation. Again, the Christian Church has Jewish and Zoroastrian roots, and those roots sprang from an earlier breakdown, the breakdown of a Syrian civilisation which was a sister to the Graeco-Roman. The kingdoms of Israel and Judah were two of the many states of this ancient Syrian world; and it was the premature and permanent overthrow of these worldly commonwealths, and the extinction of all the political hopes which had been bound up with their existence as independent politics, that brought the religion of Judaism to birth and evoked the highest expression of its spirit in the elegy of the Suffering Servant, which is appended in the Bible to the book of the prophet Isaiah. Judaism, likewise, has a Mosaic root which in its turn sprang from the withering of the second crop of the ancient Egyptian civilisation. I do not know whether Moses and Abraham are historical characters, but I think it can be taken as certain that they represent historical stages of religious experience, and Moses' forefather and forerunner, Abraham, received his enlightenment and his promise at the dissolution, in the nineteenth or eighteenth century before Christ, of the ancient

civilisation of Sumer and Akkad—the earliest case
known to us of a civilisation going to ruin. These men of
sorrows were precursors of Christ; and the sufferings
through which they won their enlightenment were
Stations of the Cross in anticipation of the Crucifixion.
That is, no doubt, a very old idea, but it is also an ever
new one . . . If religion is a chariot, it looks as if the
wheels on which it mounts towards Heaven may be
periodic downfalls of civilisations on Earth. It looks as
if the movement of civilisation may be cyclic and recurrent, while the movement of religion may be on a
single continuous upward line. The continuous upward
movement of religion may be served and promoted by
the cyclic movement of civilisations round the cycle of
birth–death–birth." [1]

There is ample corroboration of this view in the
history both of the Catholic Churches and the Protestant, of which we will consider four examples—the
mediaeval Catholic Church of the West, the Greek
Orthodox Church in Russia, and the Free Churches
both in England and the United States, especially the
Congregational Churches, and the Lutheran Church
in Germany. In each case, there was a peculiarly intimate connection between these Churches and their
respective civilisations. In each case, they are surviving
the destruction in which the civilisations have been
involved.

The relation between the Catholic Church and the
West and Feudalism was so close as very nearly to

[1] *Christianity and Civilisation*, pp, 20-2.

identify them—but not quite. If Christianity is the servant of civilisation, how can we account for the fact that the Roman Church not only survived the collapse of Feudalism, but recovered and progressed in an entirely different and alien society? For that is what has happened. In many ways Catholic Rome shaped and dominated Feudalism. Together with the Empire, it dominated mediaeval Europe. The institutions of Feudalism—its basic landed system, its armies, its political and administrative organs, its universities, its artistic activities, its monastic foundations—were almost the incarnation of the Church. They emerged and grew under the stimulus of the Church, which lived its life in them. Yet in the breakdown of Feudalism, which began roughly in the fourteenth century, down to its complete destruction in France, during the Revolution, the Church succeeded in detaching itself from its intimate body, to conquer new power and vigour in an entirely different kind of civilisation, one, moreover, so alien and hostile to it. Whatever compromise Roman Catholicism may have made with capitalism, it has never ceased to regard it as hostile. Its compromises have been on the principle of making friends with "the mammon of unrighteousness", in which art Rome has been most expert. The Papacy has amply fulfilled Lenin's conviction that, so long as you are certain of your position, you can afford to compromise. Catholic Rome survived Feudalism, just as it will survive capitalism—and recently survived Nazism, and will survive socialism, if ever it is realised. One does not need to be a Roman Catholic to admit all this. One merely needs to recognise the verdict of history. Catholic Rome survived the Holy Roman Empire (which, as has been said, was not holy nor Roman nor an empire). Feudalism dropped out of the two-legged race, but the Church shook herself free and sailed on, having got her second wind.

The Orthodox Church in Russia is an equally striking example of the same fact. Many would argue that it is even more remarkable. The close identity of the Church with the Russian State in the pre-revolutionary era was so notorious and corrupt that the word which sums it up, Byzantinism, has a more evil odour than the word Erastianism, even; which, Heaven knows, is sufficiently appalling! It became a pliable instrument in the hands of the Tsardom in the task of oppressing the various nationalities in the Empire, and of exploiting and grinding the peasant masses. The hierarchy were state officials of the worst kind. The Church gave Christian sanction to one of the worst tyrannies in modern history, and threw the cloak of sanctity over some of the worst abuses of government. That an institution guilty of such iniquity could ever survive the destruction of its partner would be a miracle. And yet that miracle has happened. That it should survive the most fanatical and determined attempt to crush it out of existence would be doubly a miracle. But that miracle has happened, too. The Soviets in their quite intelligible fury endeavoured to destroy, once and for all, what they assumed to be only a pillar of capitalist and a rival absolutist order. It looked like it. Yet their assumption was wrong. For all its evil acquiescence in the sins of a cruel régime, there was something in the Church which transcended the state and secular order, and by virtue of that secret (which Russian Communism did not realise nor will ever understand), she has experienced a new birth, a resurrection out of the murky depths of her evil past into a glorious new life. The hammer blows of an aggressive, ruthless atheistic state have succeeded in doing the very opposite of what was intended. Instead of shattering her they have welded and solidified her, until today, forty-three years after the Revolution, she is stronger than steel. In her lamps there is burning a new light which is illuminating the darkness for millions of brave souls in Russia's vast spaces. No Church in the whole world is making a richer contribution to Christian thinking and mysticism today than the Orthodox Church. But how has all this happened? The State and system to which she was wedded was shattered by the mighty blows of the October Revolution. But the Church underwent a new baptism of the Holy Ghost, to call men to repentance and hope. The most frantic activities of the anti-God society, official and State-subsidised, are powerless to silence or destroy her. Civilisation, in this instance too, has unwittingly facilitated the Church's one historic mission of bringing men to repentance.

Congregationalism, or Independency, as it was then, was intimately associated with the rise and growth of

Capitalism. The Independents were the spearhead of the Puritan revolt against the old order. They represented the new rising bourgeoisie, with their manufacturing and commercial interests. As a class they stood to benefit from the destruction of the remains of Feudalism and landed aristocracy. Right down to the nineteenth century, the manufacturing capitalists were largely nonconformist. They reflected, both in their theology and their morality, the class interests of the capitalist order. They were much more savage in their attitude to the proletariat than were the landed squires who still retained something of the paternalism of feudal relationships. The Nonconformists, among whom Congregationalists probably dominated, were thus closely bound up with capitalism—with both its practice and theory.

Now it is true that with the decline of the capitalist order, Congregationalism has undoubtedly suffered. It is experiencing great difficulty in maintaining itself, more than most Churches. It has lost considerable ground in areas in which it was once strong—in areas well known to me, Hull in the East Riding; Cardiff and the Rhondda in South Wales; Bradford in the West Riding. But he would be a rash prophet who would venture to say that, with the complete collapse of capitalism, Congregationalism would disappear as a separate force in the public life of Britain. Close as are the ties between Congregationalism and its accompanying system, it will survive its disappearance, and, in all probability, make a still finer witness to Christianity in the new age. Already there are signs that this will be so. Among its younger ministers and laymen, there is a new breath of life stirring, which is tending towards a new appreciation of its Catholic heritage. Though developing with capitalism, Congregational Christianity will survive its doom. As part of the whole Church of Christ, the breakdown of the existing order will release Congregationalism for the more effective proclamation of the Gospel of repentance.

There is, finally, the Lutheran Church in Germany. Of all the Protestant Churches, it has been particularly guilty of the sin of Erastianism, of subordinating itself to the state—and such a state as Prussia, one of whose chief makers said: "By the word 'politics' I mean that one must always try to dupe the other people . . . above all follow zealously this maxim, that to despoil your neighbours is to deprive them of the means of injuring you." Who can estimate the consequences for Europe of Martin Luther's alliance with the nobles against the peasantry in the Peasants' War? European civilisation has had to pay a stiff price in blood for the failure of the Lutheran Church to realise that Christian ethics can never be identical with those of the absolutist state.

Within the Lutheran Church, which worked so long with Prussianism and with the Nazi-controlled German Christian Movement, a new Church is arising which makes the necessity for repentance and obedience to the Word the be-all and end-all of its witness. The Confessional Church during the last war negated the tradition by which the Lutheran Church lived for so long, at a time and in a situation when it was most difficult to do so. At the moment when civilisation in Germany had become most wicked and most powerful, there arose in the Church a spirit that transcended and overcame it.

There seems to be good ground, therefore, for thinking that Dr. Toynbee's view of the relationship between Christianity and civilisation is correct. European history lends no support to the idea that Christianity is but a stepping-stone on which civilisation climbs to greater height, to finer achievement. Modern European civilisation, in fact, has not achieved greater heights, despite tremendous technical triumphs in control over matter, and in the conquest over time and space. But along with these achievements there has been a growing paralysis and self-frustration, as a result of which the technical successes are transformed into demonic destructive energies. The very evils which appear in our world are themselves the proof that Christianity transcends civilisation; since those evils correspond to the degree to which civilisation has ignored or opposed Christianity. In no previous civilisation has the assumption of human self-sufficiency, of human omnipotence, been so deep-rooted and dominating, an assumption that is the most absolute denial of the Christian revelation of man, but neither can any previous civilisation compare with it in the utter peril in which it places the whole of humanity. These two facts are not accidents, mere chances of historic process.

They are as casually related as dirt and disease. The development of civilisation, which is so largely a dialectic of disaster, is tending more and more to the recognition that future civilisation, if it is to survive, must come to terms with Christianity, must shape itself according to the Christian spirit and ethic—its power to do so is quite a different story. But what is this recognition except an admission that civilisations, in their rise and fall, are the stepping-stones to the supremacy of Christianity? History is compelling man to pay more serious heed to "the promises declared unto mankind in Christ Jesus, our Lord". History has no shelter from their power or challenge.

II

To bring the world to repentance, then, is the purpose pervading history, "according to Thy promises declared unto mankind in Christ Jesus, our Lord". The Church is the agent of Christ in history for this purpose—and the only agent. No other institution has any concern for the world's *repentance* except the Church. Other institutions are concerned, in varying degrees, to make a success of the human experiment of egocentricity. Only the Church seeks to induce repentance. The implications of this for the Church—and the world— are revolutionary. They have not yet been squarely faced.

To begin with, let us restate the primary facts of history and the Incarnation. They are extremely simple, with a grim logic uniquely their own: an issue of "Yea" or "Nay" finally inescapable, to which Anglican theology very reluctantly lends itself. *Via media* which, in a specific practical situation, may be very good sense, can be deadly in the ultimate issues. *Via media* in practice, which is not dominated and controlled at long last by something uncompromisable, is a mortal peril to the Church and the Gospel, to which she owes her first and last loyalty. What, then, are these facts which ultimately govern the Church in her historic mission? They are two.

First, man in history, the natural, unregenerate human nature is self-centred, and all civilisations, without a single exception, are attempts to make self-centredness function successfully. And so long as men remain self-centred, even in a minority, every civilisation is bound to be an experiment to make egoism a success. So long as a minority in a community is governed by self-will, the organised social life of that community cannot be any other than based on self-will; for it is impossible to coerce men into altruism. Such a civilisation may be modified by personal unselfishness, but at bottom it is itself egocentric. If this is true of the most favourable possibility, namely a community in which only a minority is self-willed, it is still more true of the less favourable possibility, namely, a society in which the majority is basically egoist. How much more true is it of a world in which no individual, Christian or non-Christian, can be said to be completely free of egoism. The least realist estimate cannot fail to recognise that civilisation today is, and tomorrow will be, an incarnation of self-will.

Lincoln said of America that it could not remain half-slave and half-free. It must be all slave or all free. Civilisation—ordered social life—cannot be half-egoistic and half-Christian. It cannot exist in isolated, insulated spheres. If egoism is its principle, it will be egoistic throughout. From that fact there is no escape. It will insinuate itself even into personal unselfishness. Like a fog, it will penetrate everywhere. Therefore, the primary fact about unredeemed man in history is that he is forever trying to make his egocentric will effective. His efforts to do this take the form of civilisation. *This is the bedrock of man in history: trying to make selfishness a success.*

The ultimate fact in the Incarnation of our Lord is the creation of a new will in man, or the recreating of his will, so that it springs from God and not from self. Christ did not attempt to reform man, to reassemble the elements of self-will into new permutations and combinations. He reorientated will to an entirely new centre, to God. Here, then, are our two ultimate facts. The fact of the world—repeated experiments to make self-will an effective principle in social relationships. The fact of the Incarnation—to replace will to self-assertion by will to affirm God. These two facts are mutually excluding. "Ye cannot serve God and Mammon." Or as St. John puts it—the love of the world and the love of the Father. "If we love the world, the love of the Father is not in us." Repentance, let it be repeated, is the first step in the reorientation of the human will from self to God.

Now if the Church is Christ's agent to proclaim repentance, she cannot share with unredeemed man his attempt to make a success of civilisation; for by her Gospel, *she knows it cannot be done*. The Church is not in the world to improve human nature, but to redeem it. The commission given to the Church by Christ was not to make men better, but to save them. It is not because a man is a bad man that he is sinful. It is possible to be a decent citizen, husband, and parent, never guilty of dishonesty or unchastity or disloyalty or any big sin, yet be dead in sin in the Gospel sense. It is possible to be a good Churchman, to have the best possible reputation, even to think oneself a reasonably good man, yet to be dead in sin. It is even possible to be worried about one's sins yet remain dead in sin. It is the function of the Church to make men conscious of sin and of the need for repentance. It is no part of the Church's task in history, therefore, to attempt to make a success of civilisation, to make human nature in its unregenerate condition, work. The world is obsessed by the illusion, especially in periods of crisis like the present, that new ventures in social rebuilding can succeed, where others have failed. It is true, of course, the new social development does effect technical, social solutions of economic or political or social problems. But these solutions are never radical or final. The problems present themselves in new forms and have to be solved all over again. Human nature, being dynamic, will breed new perils to peace and justice. In that illusion the Church cannot share, if she is to be faithful to her commission. Making human nature work is the world's impossible task. The Church's business is to revolutionise it by repentance for redemption.

Has the Church, then, nothing to do with the social order? Has the Church no contribution to make to the vast social and political problems which are pressing the world today? Has she no obligation to try to secure justice, to mitigate the great evils that oppress the world in its economic, political and social relationships? Is it, or ought it to be, a matter of indifference to the Church how escape is made from the threat of war? If repentance of persons is the task of the Church, does it not mean that the Church must let the social order go hang? However logical such a conclusion may *appear* to be, it is nevertheless profoundly anti-Christian. But even the logic is one of appearance only, if but for the reason that the person whom the Church calls to repentance is indissolubly linked to the social order, which is the sum total of individuals *in relation*.

The degeneration of Luther's theology into the doctrine that the Gospel was irrelevant to the state and world-order was a perverted expression of a profound truth. It reflected, of course, the increasing subordination of Luther to the German princes on whose assistance he had relied in his struggle against the Papacy. His doctrine was inspired much more by the class interests of the German nobility than by the New

Testament. Imbedded in it, however, was a deep in-tuition, namely, that a Christian society could not be realised in this world of time and space. The world can never be the habitation of the Kingdom of God in its fullness and power. But, pushed by his alliance with the princes, Luther concluded too much. Since the Kingdom's destiny is in heaven, it can have no place on earth. And that was Luther's great error, which has accumulated a damnable heritage for Germany and Europe.

It is difficult to comprehend the bearing of Christianity on social order unless one grasps the idea that it is a tension of opposites, that it involves doing opposite things at the same time. We cannot understand Christianity by static thinking. The comprehension of Christianity demands the dialectical mind. In this question of the primacy of repentance, the Church, on the one hand, has no concern with civilisation; on the other hand, it has a profound obligation, *to the Gospel*, to secure justice, and to co-operate with the world in the development and progress of civilisation. A brief consideration of the Pauline doctrine of the Law will, perhaps, help to make this clear.

The Jewish Law (Torah), said St. Paul, was the schoolmaster to bring the Jew to Christ. It was the disciplinary process through which the Jew would learn that the demands made upon him by the Law could, at last, be satisfied only by Christ. The Law set him a task, the impossibility of which he would dis-cover in the honest attempt to perform it. This was the deep-rooted but grand tragedy in the experience of St. Paul himself. After a lifetime of passionate, whole-hearted effort to fulfil the Law's demands St. Paul at the last is broken by the bitter realisation that the task is beyond his power. "How unhappy am I! Who will make me free from the body of this death", [1] i.e. this contradiction of feeling that I must try to do something in spite of the fact that I cannot do it.

But the Jew only discovers the impossibility of the task by attempting it. Had St. Paul taken the line that, since the Law was impossible of realisation, it was therefore foolish to try, he would never have discovered the fact *for himself, and so would not have come to Christ*. It was a dialectic. Here is an objective which the Jew feels compelled to realise. In the pursuit of it he learns that he can never attain it. But it is that very same bitter discovery which reveals to him how it can be achieved. It is in the bitter proof of his own moral impotence that he comes to Christ. God ordained the Law, says St. Paul, as the means whereby the Jew may learn that its satisfaction can be effected, not by himself, but only by Christ. His pride is so profound and stubborn that only his failure can convince him of his powerlessness. The proof of the pudding is in the actual eating. Even then he won't believe. He has to become ruminant and re-eat what he has already swallowed ere he finally repents.

The illusion that civilisation can be made to progress permanently is to the modern man what the Law was

[1] This is the Basic English rendering of Romans vii, verse 24.

to the Jew. The attempt to make it so is the discipline by which civilised man has to learn that the power to realise it is beyond him. The thing, of course, is a contradiction. On the one hand there is the moral pressure of the obligation which men feel to secure justice in social relationships, to effect progress in historical development, to raise civilisation to new heights of technical achievement, to more stable political foundations, to a more humane economic system. This categorical imperative all men feel, irrespective of whether they are Christian or not. It is the equivalent of the Torah to the Jew, of the Natural Law of the Stoic and the Roman lawyers. On the other hand, there is the incompatibility of the instrument for doing it— the balancing of conflicting egoisms, which, being dynamic, never permits any settlement to stay put. The failure in actual practice is the bitter school in which man is placed to learn, at last, that the ideal to which he is compulsorily attracted cannot be achieved by egocentric will. Through that realisation he may come to repentance and the acceptance of Christ.

Since, then, the attempt to do the impossible is the divinely ordained discipline of the human race for redemption, it is surely clear that the Church, as the historic agent of God's will to save man, must encourage and promote that discipline. How can the Church discharge her obligation to her Lord in this matter, if she holds aloof from the social problem? The Church, quite plainly, must participate in attempts to do the impossible, since such attempts constitute the human process in which man will come to repentance, a process ordained of God. God does not, of Himself, will that man should suffer and sin, but He does will that man should be a free moral agent. Since He wills men to be free, then the toleration of the human illusion that Utopia is a human possibility comes within the providence of God. And that which is within the providence of God is also within the sphere of the Church's obligation. God permits what He knows will collapse. The Church must co-operate in what she knows will not succeed, because the experience of failure will—may—bring repentance. The realisation by man of the significance of *historic* failure is spiritual success. Man's failure, when taken to heart, is God's justification, God's success. Hence the Church is under divine obligation to urge man, on the one hand, to secure justice, and on the other hand, to convince him of the meaning of his proved failure to do so.

To this argument, the reader may respond by saying that, surely, it is cynical to expect the Church to do what she knows is going to fail. To give a concrete case, can it be seriously argued that the Church should co-operate with unregenerate man to participate in the struggle to institute a new social order to distribute wealth, to reduce poverty, to multiply cultural facilities, to secure world-peace, to improve human standards, when she knows that none of these things will really touch the fundamental problem; when indeed she knows that these things, in their turn, will give rise to new evils? Isn't this a counsel of immoral, cynical indifference? Yes, *if the only object of the Church is to rejoice in failure.* But if the object of the Church is *to utilise the failure of man for his own redemption and the glory of God,* then her counsel, her Gospel, is anything but one of cynicism. On the contrary, it becomes one of the profoundest concern for man, and faith in God. Were those great religious seers who urged the Jew to obey the demands of the Law cynical, when they knew that the utmost obedience would still fail to satisfy the "Law's demands"? Was St. Paul a cynic? What the Church, by her Gospel, looks to, is not merely the failure of man to realise his dreams of good, but the possibility, through his failure, to discover Christ, who will more than fulfil man's noblest dream.

Another objection which the reader may advance is that to expect men to work sincerely and enthusiastically for European regeneration, for a new civilisation, with the belief that it will all be frustrated is hopeless psychology. It is difficult enough, in the best of circumstances, to realise ideals of social justice. Men can only be got to promote social progress if they are animated by a spirit of hope, by a belief that their labour will not be in vain. If you begin by telling them that their efforts are to be disappointed, they will not respond. And then what will happen?

It is true, of course, that men would not set about the task of building a new world if they believed that their new civilisation would become a breeding-ground of new evils. *If they believed it.* But this is precisely what the humanist, secularised, non-Christian mind of today does not believe. I wish it did! And no amount of tell-ing will convince. The actual experiencing of it will have to be gone through—again and again. In every day of social rebuilding, hope soars with unfettered wing. *This* new civilisation will succeed! That is the attitude of the humanist, though less confident as time goes on. The reader need have no fear that the argu-ment presented here is likely to paralyse unregenerate man. His pride still stands firmly. It will take more than a couple of world-wars to knock that down. Of course, it may temporarily paralyse Christians who hitherto have been indulging in humanist illusions about the perfectibility of human nature and the inevitability of progress. But they will recover.

Is it too much to expect that Christian men and women who have faith in Christ, a resource not ex-ploited by the natural man, should be able to work with the world for something that cannot be realised by the world? For the sake of human redemption? But that would be cynicism, and of the worst kind. That would be to demand that "the promises declared unto mankind in Christ Jesus, our Lord" are worthless, unless they are going to be implemented completely here in time, in this world. In this matter, Christians can take a leaf out of the book of the convinced revolutionist. In the course of his examination in Mexico by a distinguished commission under the chairmanship of John Dewey, the late Leon Trotsky, that revolutionary petrel of revolution, said: "I have patience. Three revolutions have made me patient. It is absolutely necessary for a revolutionist to be patient. It is a false idea that a revolutionary must be impatient. Adventurists are impatient, but a revolutionary is patient. . . . It is on this false idea of a revolutionary that all the frame-ups are based: 'Trotsky wants power. He is impatient. He will kill everybody to take power.' This is absolutely stupid. I am not hungering for power personally. I am more satisfied with my literary work. Power is a burden, but it is necessary and an inevitable evil . . . I am patient and await a new wave, a revolutionary wave." [1] If three revolutions taught Trotsky to be patient, whose hopes were limited to time, should not experience teach Christians, whose hopes are not bounded by time, to be at least as patient? God has all eternity in which to move and work His sovereign will. Man's failure is working to His glory. So what is certainly an impossible psychology for men who have not the resources of faith in God is more than possible for those who have seen God in Christ.

It is the Church's obligation, then, to her Gospel to be greatly concerned with the social problem in all its aspects. The Church, in other words, and as has so frequently been said, is to act in society as a social conscience. That is, at every step she is to remind society that, even when it has done its utmost and best, it still falls short—and no society ever does its utmost and best. But even if it did, the Church, in her witness, has to proclaim that the world's best is never good

[1] *The Case of Leon Trotsky*, p. 278 (Secker & Warburg, 1937).

enough. What does this mean except that it is not within the power of man to do what he ought to do, to create a just society, to secure civilisation against the contradiction of self-will? But let man go on trying and he will discover the truth, which leads to repentance. If man's best is not good enough, then the problem, *as far as man is concerned,* is settled. The necessary best has to be sought elsewhere—in God, who has already provided it in Christ. Indeed, the Church must act as conscience for the world.

To fulfil this function the Church must be possessed of insight into historic process and development. Lack of it has frequently made the Church, not the conscience which stabs, but a power of reaction to resist and hinder the forces of historic progress. Much of Church history makes very melancholy reading for anyone who takes Christ seriously; for too often, alas! the Church has displayed blindness to the meaning of events, and thus failed to interpret the signs of the time. The real failure of the Church is, not that it hasn't made society or even herself Christian, but that, only too frequently, she has allowed society and herself to confuse Christianity with paganism. Her failure, in other words, has been more prophetic than ethical. And by identifying Christianity with the established order or with her own institutional interests (which, while serving the Gospel, also oppose it very often), she has degenerated into a soporific. This is the real charge against the Church. We can illustrate this by a brief consideration of the attitude of the Church in general, and the Roman Church in particular, towards socialism, especially Marxian socialism.

To begin with, the demand that the Church should espouse socialism—so passionately made by the Christian socialists—on the ground that socialism is the ethical embodiment of Christianity is inspired, in my judgment, by a profound misunderstanding of the New Testament Gospel. In rejecting that demand, the Church showed a much surer and deeper instinct than the Christian socialist. No humanism can ever be the ethical embodiment of Christianity. Only the Kingdom of God can ever be that. And the Kingdom does not come by "observation", that is, by organisation, movements, legislation and revolutions. The confusion of Christianity with socialism is the peculiar blindness of the Left. But in refusing that demand, the Church also closed her mind to the historic prophetic element in socialism. She threw the baby out along with the bath-water. She failed to detect in socialism that element in it which was significant of judgment, of divine judgment.

The Roman Church, which felt the foetid breath of the atheism so predominant in the European socialist movement, condemned the whole of it lock, stock and barrel, as any reader can see for himself by a study of the Papal encyclicals, *Rerum Novarum* and *Quadragesimo Anno*. But she failed to appreciate the historic significance of socialism, that it was a signal of the approaching end of the capitalist order. The end of a social order is always a sign of Providence in action. The emergence of socialism in European politics was a symptom, not merely of discontent, but of something much more important. It was a sign that capitalist civilisation was coming to the point at which its contribution to progress would cease. That is, from the point of view of Providence in history, its value as historic, moral discipline of man for repentance was being exhausted. A social system which fetters the forces of progress and consequently is concerned only with its own perpetuation, has lost its moral value as well as its social. A system which *resists* progress serves only to strengthen the human illusion of omnipotence; for obviously men think that the disintegrating system is the root of their problem. To perpetuate a system which is historically exhausted is to fortify men in delusion and error. The pioneers of democracy believed that Absolutism was the root of war; that democracy would mean peace. We know better, *because absolutism has given way to democracy.* Today, it is said, capitalism is the root of war: socialism will mean peace. It will, of course, mean nothing of the kind. But the great danger is that the world will not believe that until the whole world has tried it. Capitalism means war, and, now that it has exhausted its capacity to promote social progress, it will mean war more than ever. The moral and spiritual discipline it imposed upon society has finished. It is this profound fact that the emergence of socialism, specially Marxian socialism, signifies. And it is this fact, too, which the wholesale hostility of the Roman Church has failed to appreciate.

The Protestant Churches have been equally slow to appreciate it. The Free Churches, as we have already indicated, reflected to an alarming degree the spirit and morality of capitalism, which is one reason why, from the 'seventies onwards, they lost more and more of their adherents to the trade union and socialist movements. They were deaf to the accents of Providence in the socialist movement. In the middle years of the last century, it was Marx, much more than most Christian thinkers, who sensed the beginning of disintegration in capitalism.[1] But Marx was born of a nation which had specialised in prophets. His insight derived at least as much from his prophetic blood as from Hegelianism. When as yet there were few outward signs of the coming collapse, Marx sensed it coming. It was the Church that should have done so, but didn't. She will act most searchingly and powerfully as the conscience of society, when she recovers and exercises her *prophetic* function, the witness to man that God's judgment is operating in events.

Secular movements, while they express the dynamic of free human self-will, are also vehicles of God's judgment. The Church is swift to recognise the one, but often slow in sensing the other. The Roman Church, for example, realised the danger which the atheism of Bolshevism spelled to Europe. But there was an element of judgment in Bolshevism too, as there was in Nazism. But Catholic Rome's obsession with the dan-

[1] Dostoievsky was a notable exception. His insight was much deeper than that of Marx.

ger dulled her sense of the judgment. She was much slower in seeing that than the Orthodox Church, which, after the Revolution, saw that element in Bolshevism very clearly.[1] The same thing was true about the Roman attitude to the Civil War in Spain. They sensed the peril to the Church and to civilisation of the utter secularism of the Spanish Republicans. But she showed little evidence of being aware of the even greater peril to Europe of a Catholic triumph made possible—and only made possible—by Nazi and Fascist guns and planes. But Rome has always tended to identify the Kingdom with the Church. To defend the Church is therefore to defend the Kingdom of God. *But that is frequently untrue.*

It is by prophetic insight that the Church can best discharge her social obligation to the Gospel and the world. And prophetic insight comes from dependence on the Bible as the Living Word of God. Not the Bible as the instrument for developing the faculty of critical analysis or "designed to be read as literature", but as the work of the Spirit which brooks no denial. The Bible has pronounced sentence on every civilisation, before it comes to birth. To nurture herself in and on the Bible, therefore, is to deliver herself forever from sharing human illusions about unredeemed man. Nothing penetrates into the inner core of events like the Bible. And the prophecies are more up-to-date than *The Times*, and also profounder in their interpretation

---

[1] Berdyaev's chapter on the Russian revolution in his *The End of Our Time* (Sheed & Ward, 1933).

of politics, even of the politics of the twentieth century.
Let the Church feed on the Bible, and she will become
sensitive to the operation of divine judgment in the
world.

III

To bring men and women to repentance—that is the
supreme objective of the Church, since it is the transcendent purpose dominating history. "Repent ye; for
the Kingdom of God is at hand." Since the resurrection
of Jesus Christ, the Kingdom of God has always been
at hand. Hence, the paradox of repentance is that it
consummates history in history. It is not something
which only happens at the end of a long process in
time. It telescopes the historic process each time it
happens. When one individual truly repents, there
history comes to fulfilment in that individual.

And it is individuals that repent. Repentance is
essentially personal, not institutional. It is aristocratic,
not democratic. It is personal, aristocratic and spiritual.
The final abandonment of self-will, while its effects and
consequences go beyond time and history, can be
essentially realised here and now—which is only another
way of saying that the life eternal, the life which takes
its rise out of God, is a reality in time. It does not mean
that humanity has to exhaust its dynamic self-will before repentance can be experienced. Men can and do
repent now. Since our Lord's life, death and resurrection, men have repented and found God. And in spite

of all the terrible secularisation of mind and heart which the Western World has undergone, men and women, unseen by the world, unreported by journalists, unannounced by the radio, have descended the abyss of self-despair and come face to face with God, and have resurrected to new and triumphant life. God's promise of new life, of new being, in Christ is being carried out here and everywhere, now and always.

In the past, the pre-Christian era, God dealt with nations and peoples as collectives. His dealing with the individual was as a unit subordinate to the collective. God deals still with nations, but directly with individual persons. "But you are a special people, a holy nation," says the first epistle of Peter, "because you have had a new birth, not from the seed of man, but from eternal seed, through the word of a living and unchanging God." [1] A holy nation! How has this new nation come into being? Through the repentance of individual persons out of every nation and race. It is a community of people in whom self-consciousness functions within communal realisation, and communal realisation intensifies personal consciousness. God's Kingdom shall not be complete until all people have become part of this new nation. God rests not day or night for the consummation of that grand design, which is the promise that He has "declared unto mankind in Christ Jesus, our Lord".

[1] Chapter ii, verse 9, and Chapter i, verse 23. The translation is from the Basic New Testament (C.U.P.).

Seven

THE ETHICAL CONSEQUENCE
OF THEOLOGY

*"That we may hereafter live a godly, righteous and
sober life."*

IT WILL SURELY BE CLEAR TO THE READER, AT THIS
stage of our argument, that there can be no repentance
without theology. Men, of course, can feel sorrow or
regret over wrong which they have done, and determine to live differently without any theology. But, as
we have seen, repentance is far different, far more
profound, than just feeling sorry and determining to
do better. Repentance is realisation with one's whole
being that what one is is wrong, that one's whole life
is an offence to a Holy God; that one's total being, the
instinctive natural self-will, is a violation of God's will
and love. Repentance, therefore, is a theological, as
well as a moral, psychological and spiritual fact. How
can a man *repent* unless he believes; (*a*) in the existence
of God; (*b*) that God created man perfect in freedom;
(*c*) that by using his freedom to rebel against God,
man fell from his original state; (*d*) that it is God's will,
declared in Christ, that man should abandon his self-
will for God's will? These beliefs, theological beliefs,
constitute an absolutely necessary minimum before any

man can *repent*. The General Confession is incurably theological, saturated through and through by theology —and by a severely orthodox, uncompromising theology. Ample evidence has been offered in these pages to show that the General Confession is also political, economic, cultural—that is, sociological in the widest sense. But before all these, and deeper than these, it is theological. Which is merely another way of saying that theology is intensely relevant to political and social problems, that it has profound economic and political implications. Theology had a great deal to do in the creating of Feudalism. It also had a great deal to do with the making of capitalism, as Max Weber, and his English disciple, R. H. Tawney, have so conclusively demonstrated. Back of the entire historic process is theology. This is the revolutionary significance of the General Confession. The act of revolution is personal repentance. Its determining, decisive factor is theology.

The consequences of it all are ethical, moral. Theology is profoundly ethical in character. "That we may hereafter *live* a godly, righteous and sober life." In its essence, theology is a combination of theory and practice. Marx was not the first, by a very long way, to relate dialectically those two activities. There can be no revolution, said Lenin, without a theory of revolution. He was not the first to realise the organic connection between the two. It is interesting to observe how St. Paul, especially in his epistles to Romans and Galatians (which are the great theological epistles), develops his theological argument, without any artificial jerks, to

187

an ethical conclusion. Mighty theological principles and issues move in a straight line to practical moral decisions and acts—"feed the hungry", "love the brethren", "owe no man anything", etc. Whatever form of knowledge or science can remain in isolation from the practical issues and concerns of life, theology cannot and, in fact, never does. A bad or wrong theology inevitably involves a vicious practice.

Before men can, therefore, come to repentance, they must become theological. Our generation will rediscover theology by being forced to recognise the theological character of the political and economic issues involved in the making of a new world. But precisely by such a theological rediscovery, our time will also come to a new ethic of personal and social being.

I

A popular topic of debate is, does it matter what a man believes? And the incredible but constant answer is that it does not matter what a man believes, so long as he acts rightly. Conduct, apparently, has no relation to belief. Ethics have nothing to do with theology. The explosion of this antiquated idea by history itself makes no difference whatever to those holding such ideas who think the Christian ethic can be divorced from Christian theology and be remarried to secular socialism. Adultery, for instance, when legalised, can be made respectable. Fond delusion! Doctrine doesn't matter. Pitch it overboard. It is like a buyer in a slave-market. Here are slaves sold in pairs—one of the pair old, ugly and weak; the other beautiful and young. The customer insists on buying only the one. Let the slave-dealer do what he likes with the other. So our contemporary good pagans and humanists have belatedly discovered the virtue of Christian ethics and propose to adopt it without the doctrine. For our present-day humanists, or our near-Marxists to argue (as they do) that you can divorce Christian ethical principles from Christian theology is like saying that you can institute a proletarian revolution by the instrumentation of conservative political theory; that you can derive Communism in practice from Burke in theory. That men can make Christian ethical principles work as the obedient slaves of a theologically securarised society is the dandiest of all delusions.

What men believe is overwhelmingly important, especially in the long run. In a very real sense, what men believe is even more important than what they do. The Catholic evaluation of the significance of heresy is profoundly right, just as right as the Catholic persecution of heresy was wrong. Lecky's argument that the Church's idea of the supreme importance of doctrine for the eternal destiny of the soul necessarily involves intolerance and persecution, holds good only when we forget dialectic, that illogical opposites can exist side by side. Christianity holds both the idea that doctrine is decisive for human destiny *and also* that there must be freedom to believe and propagate erroneous doctrine; for only by freedom to be in error can men ultimately come to believe and realise the truth. What our generation is beginning to suspect is not the decisiveness of the doctrine concerning an order beyond death (which is not in its reckoning, not on its agenda), but the decisiveness of Christian doctrine for civilisation, for the future of Europe and the world here and now. There is an awakening of the idea, in unlikely quarters, that Christian principles (so-called) are of vital importance for the future of society. It goes under the name of "a revival of Christian values". The degradation into which the Western World has fallen since the last war; the loosening of all restraints upon power-politics; the complete a-morality to which the conflict has reduced national relationships have violently jerked the secularised progressive mind of today into the belated discovery that there is a very close connection between Christianity and European culture and civilisation. When they see these going down the abyss of a new and unprecedented barbarism, they suddenly develop a new appreciation of Christian values. This is the first step to the realisation of the significance of Christian theology, but only a first step. The non-Christian mind, however, is still obsessed with the notion that the revival of Christian values will be facilitated if the Church abandons orthodox dogma. That is altogether a reactionary idea in the perilous situation in which Europe finds itself today. In any case it is untrue and impossible. One thing is certain: that the Church will never abandon the dogmas on which her faith rests—those dogmas which according to some people no thinking person can ever again be persuaded to believe. To throw away dogma would be to destroy the final barrier which is stemming the tide of naked materialism rising over Europe, entrenched in America and spreading over the rest of the world. Dogma, so far from being a fetter upon Christian ethics, is its foundation and defence.

This plea from the secular progressives for the separation of ethics from dogma is the form which human pride takes in a disintegrating society. It is the response of a disillusioned society, still refusing to repent, to the dissipation of its hopes and beliefs. Whilst capitalist Europe was still on the upward grade, still progressing, still promising to fulfil the Utopian illusions of men, as it appeared to be doing until a few generations ago, Christian dogma was despised and made ridiculous in the eyes of thinking men. And Christian ethics was ignored. So great was the pressure of the secular mind's contempt of dogma on Christian thinkers and theologians, that, in Liberal Protestantism, an attempt was made to accommodate theology to the prejudices and assumptions of secularised modern thought—an attempt compounded of a conscious dealing with genuine intellectual difficulties of faith, and an unconscious feeling of inferiority to modern thought, due, I believe, to a withering of Christian experience, or at least to its becoming thin and shallow. And Christian ethics were presented as statements of purely secular social processes, as expressions of what the world was, in fact, actually doing. The economic and political co-operation of classes and nations (e.g. in the International Labour Office) an historc by-product (i.e. partly automatic and wholly institutional) of capitalist development, was made equivalent to Christian love and brotherhood. Many Liberal theologians, especially American, in their enthusiasm for what was called "the Social Gospel", grew positively lyrical in their appreciation of international finance, as embodying mutual trust and co-operation. Credit and the world money market became symbols of modern man's automatic realisation of Christian principles.[1] The International Rotary Movement organised this new worship. But all this happened in an unclouded era of expansion— unclouded as contrasted with a later era of stress and collapse—and still alive even in this day of even greater expansion, though now charged through and through with trembling fears.

The cruel awakening from these dreams into the stark bloody reality of our recent experiences, revealed these romantic, arrogant constructions for the shallow nonsense that they were, empty of the slightest realisation of the tragedy of human nature. Christian ethics are now something to be *recovered*. International financiers are not, it seems, Christian priests disguised in perfectly-creased trousers and immaculate silk ties; they are, on the contrary, the all-powerful hierarchy of "Acquisitive Society", sick to death with its acquisitiveness. Back, therefore, to Christian principles of

[1] Consult, e.g., the earlier works of Francis Peabody, Dr. Shailer Matthews, and Bruce Barton's *The Man Nobody Knew*, etc.

conduct! But draw the line at dogma! Like the French *sansculotte*, who drew the line exactly between the head and the body. "Ethics only need apply."

What is the assumption behind this plea? It is as plain as a pikestaff.

It is that modern man, secularised, still too profound a thinker to accept Christian dogma, without repentance, without despairing abandonment of pride and humble submission to Christ, can, by his own power and determination, practise Christian ethics. It is that men can live by the Christian spirit without being born again, about the necessity for which the New Testament speaks with one clear voice. It is the assumption that by a decision of will, *still unredeemed*, men can become naturally, instinctively altruistic instead of instinctively egoistic, primarily self-regarding. What is this but original sin, the peacock's feathers of human pride all over again? Well! the answer is brief. *It can't be done.* If our generation will not accept this assurance, it is preparing a still more terrible heritage for its children and children's children, compared to which the dreaded bombs will look like instruments of mercy. We must repent, which necessitates acceptance of dogma, if we want to "live hereafter a godly, righteous and sober life".

II

"Hereafter" does not mean only future time. It means the eternity beyond time as well. The complete sloughing off of the old Adam is a process impossible to telescope into the years of man's life. It may be possible, as the advertisements so confidently tell us, to compress an ox into a pot of Bovril, about which one may be reasonably doubtful without being cynical. But we cannot be doubtful about the fact that, what the New Testament calls "sanctification", is a process beyond the capacity of time to exhaust. After repentance, with its dogmatic pre-requisite, it begins. Yea, indeed and indeed it begins. And it continues, spite of pain, relapse and failure, throughout the rest of our earthly span. It runs on into a new plane of being, beyond the tears and defeats of mortality.

> *Brief life is here our portion;*
> *Brief sorrow, short-lived care;*
> *The life that knows no ending,*
> *The tearless life is there.*

> *And now we fight the battle,*
> *But then shall wear the crown*
> *Of full and everlasting*
> *And passionless renown.*

The eternal life, to know God, begins here and goes on finally to burst time into fuller, richer being.

"That we may hereafter live a godly, righteous, and sober life." To repent is to resurrect. That is what history is for. The most important thing in life today is not to create a new world society, but to learn how to die, so that we may be sure of resurrection. The creation of a new world is certainly important, but it derives its importance from the supreme end of dying aright—"that we may hereafter live a godly, righteous and sober life". What, in essence, is the godly, righteous, sober life?

(*a*) The Godly life is a life that takes its rise out of the will of God, as contrasted with the life that originates from individual or collective self-will. God and Self are the two forces that seek to divide the empire of life between them. This is what St. John means when he writes of "the world" and "the Father". They are forever opposed and distinct. Though they may interpenetrate, yet they never merge into one. Never! "Love not the world, neither the things that are in the world. If any man love the world, the love of the Father is not in him. For all that is in the world, the lust of the flesh, the lust of the eyes, and the pride of life, is not of the Father, but is of the world. And the world passeth away, and the lust thereof: but he that doeth the will of God abideth forever." [1] The godly man is one in whose mind God thinks, in whose heart God suffers and feels, in whose will God acts. This does not imply that the godly man is an automaton, as it might superficially seem to do. God does not displace individuality. Rather does He intensify it. In the truly godly life, the individual heart, mind and will become so closely identified with God's will and being, that a man lives God—independently, spontaneously and freely. It is the mystics who can tell us most about the

[1] 1st St. John ii, 15–17.

godly life; for it is they who have anticipated in time the richer development of union with God, which, for the majority of men, will be realised only beyond time.

Since the godly life originates from God, since its source is the will of God, it is clearly the expression of a new relation to God, with a new purpose, new values, a new destiny. "Every man in Christ is a new creation." Consequently, the world—the order of convention and social striving—loses its power. The World's power over man lies in the fact that men, in their innermost souls, believe in it and passionately crave its goods and prizes. Not for nothing does St. John bid us not to love the world. But the antidote to love of the world is love of the Father. Love of the Father is the Johannine mode of expression for the godly life, entrance to which is effected by repentance. This is the key to the new life, the re-discovery by man of his primal ralation to God.

(*b*) *The righteous life* is the social aspect of man's personal relation to God. It is the expression in human relationships of the new status in which the individual stands towards God. If we may characterise the godly life as *mystical*, then we may say that the righteous life is *social*. It is the same life in a different aspect.

The basic element in righteousness is justice—i.e. the right relations between man and man. Society is seeking after this by a method which can never achieve it; which is to attempt to balance conflicting and ultimately irreconcilable claims. War is the symbol of the ultimate, non-possumus point in society. War is the final logic of self-will. Human justice embodies the ideal of love in a compulsory form. That is, it contradicts it, for the claim of love can never be realised by coercion. A point is reached when men will not give way or compromise. A situation is reached where claims can no longer be balanced. Marx understood this very well. In the final analysis, the just claim is conceded by the abolition of the opposition—and that contains the seed of new justice, which Marx understood less clearly.

In history, then, because of self-will, man is driven to realise right relations by the negating method of coercion. And so long as egoism predominates, he has no alternative. This is where pacifism is romantic. It assumes or implies as a social fact, what does not exist—the natural transcendence of egoism. Even when it recognises egoism as an all-pervading factor, it then assumes something equally romantic—that egoism can be abolished by an effort of natural will, as the last war disproved more conclusively than any war in history. Thus, justice is never, in fact, achieved.

By the abandonment of egoistic will, which repentance initiates as a concrete possibility, right relations in society come about spontaneously. When the members of a society all stand in the same relation to a central, transcendent Will, then their individual wills harmonise—not by organisation, but by spontaneous attraction. And that is true justice. Only Love can achieve justice.

(*c*) *The sober life* must not be confused with total abstinence. It is a fairly safe guess that the divines, who composed the General Confession under the inspiration of the Holy Ghost, were far too appreciative of good ale and wine to make the mistake of thinking that the divine life in man meant the exclusion of good gifts of God. This is not the place to argue the merits or demerits of total abstinence, which is a different thing from temperance—its opposite, in fact. But it may be pointed out that its principle, if generally applied, would mean the cessation of history: that because alcoholic liquors are abused, they should be forbidden altogether.[1] *But every material thing in a sin-dominated world is abused.* Sex, for example. Shall we then organise a movement to secure total abstinence from sexual intercourse?

The sober life is a controlled life, the perfectly balanced and co-ordinated life, in which all man's faculties and dynamic, creative powers are developed to the full *in relation to one another.* So it is really an intoxicated life, a God-intoxicated life. It is something very different from the Greek ideal of everything in moderation. It is rather everything in excess, in abundance, in tropical profusion. "Love God—and do as you will", when one's will proceeds out of the love of God. The "sober life" of the General Confession is a fully-proportioned life, not one-sided and ill-balanced. Men don't become all intellect and feeble heart; or all

[1] The late G. K. Chesterton, the most lovable defender of beer in English literature, used to reply, when told that to drink alcohol was injurious, that he never drank alcohol. He merely drank beer.

will and no brains; or all heart and no will or intellect. Neither do they live at half-cock, or travel in low gear. The sober life, in the crisp Americanism, "steps on it". It goes all out. "They shall have life, *and have it more abundantly*." Isaac Watts must have been aware of this profound truth, when he deplored that "we live at this poor dying rate". Nothing is a greater caricature of Christian living than devitalised Christians.

Thus the new life to which repentance opens the door is a rich, full life. The Christian should be the most comprehensive of all people. He should be mystical, social and dynamic. Godly—righteous—and sober; here is the trinity of Christian character.

And this is the consequence of theology! In the final analysis, theology is profoundly ethical.

Eight

THE ADORATION OF THE REDEEMED

"To the glory of Thy Holy Name. Amen."

THIS IS THE GRAND, ECSTATIC FINALE OF OUR confession. At long last, here is the transcendent objective of all cosmic existence—to render homage to the glory of God. In this do the redeemed find the end of living. History is the tragic antithesis which finds its final synthesis in the ecstatic worship of God, which is human awareness of the divine glory. Here is man's true function. We glorify God not only with our minds and our bodies but with our essential selves, the self we have abandoned and received again from Him.

Among the absolute values of secular thought worship, of course, finds no place. Each of these values, in fact, is not absolute, for they do not absorb the ego, but intensify its contradictions. An absolute activity is one that obsesses and absorbs individuality without dissolving it into non-being. An activity is not absolute which, in intensifying self-consciousness, merely heightens the inner contradictions of self-conscious individuality, merely makes the self more aware of its opposing non-self. An absolute activity must fulfil

self-conscious individuality, transcend the inner contradictions, intensify self-consciousness of the self and,
at the same time, intensify the consciousness of the
non-self *as part of the self*. Only Christianity can do that
as communion with God, as mystical activity, as worship, which even in the flesh, in time with all its
stresses and frictions, can give even the most elementary Christian a foretaste of Paradise. The most imperfect of Christians can surely recall one experience of
worship in which, for a flash, he transcended himself.
It only happens in religion, because there man senses
the glory of God.

The secular cult of self-realisation ends in dust and
ashes. That particular absolute is the most hollow of all
shams. Concentrated on itself, the ego can never escape
itself. And without escape from self there can be no
absolute. Let us take culture as an example, in its
widest sense as a cultivation of personality. It is necessarily a cultivation of self-contradiction. It isolates men
from one another if they are culturally divergent from
one another. How rare it is for highly cultivated
people, even at their best, to find fellowship with
uncultured people. And by fellowship I do not mean
sitting for an hour over a pint of beer, but consciousness
of something common which deprives cultural achievement of any element of pride. At its worst, as we used
to find it in Bloomsbury, for example, cultural
achievement leads to contempt. Here again, in the
worship of God by renewed, regenerated souls, whatever their differences, cultural or social, they find in the

glory of God the common reality in which differences between people no longer isolate, but unite them.

To worship God, to meditate on Him, to contemplate His glory is the supreme end and the highest activity of man redeemed and purified. "What is man's chief end?" asks the Westminster Shorter Catechism and answers—"Man's chief end is to glorify God and to enjoy Him forever." Hence, the whole of human life, its economic, political, social and cultural pursuits, if man is ever to realise himself fully, must be invested with worship. It must be organised, and developed as an offering to the glory of God. The glory of God must become the prime and only motive of human activity. This can never be achieved in time by sinful man. But the glory of God as the impelling motive of civilisation can be made the standard of judgment, so that men be kept forever humble.

Europe has known a time when such a motive was partially operative. The age which built the great cathedrals, for instance, was not unaware of the reality of the glory of God. Without falling to the temptation of idealising the mediaeval craftsman, who was very human, we can, nevertheless, state that there was dedication in his work. Mediaeval life was organised round the Church, more particularly in the manor and village. Men lived and worked with the thought that it was their service to God. And that temper and attitude must be recovered. Human activities must be constantly referred to this standard: can they be offered to God as an expression of worship? It is surely unnecessary to argue that such a standard of reference for social activities, even perfunctorily and imperfectly applied, would make a tremendous difference to the spirit and temper of civilisation. It would certainly help to make the public conscience a little more acute. It would become more difficult to live on rents from slum property, for example, without greater discomfort. "To the glory of Thy Holy Name," applied to civilisation, would be the most revolutionary of all principles.

Meanwhile, in the midst of sinful history, the Church witnesses to the glory of God in her activity of worship which has a twofold significance. First, through worship, the Church on earth joins with the redeemed of God everywhere in what is the essential activity of the Kingdom of God—rendering glory to God. In worship redeemed souls, both on earth and in Heaven, become one community. This is supremely effected in the Mystery of the Body and the Blood. In the sacrament of Holy Communion redeemed souls fuse into community. "Therefore with Angels and Archangels and all the company of Heaven we"— still on earth—"laud and magnify Thy glorious name; evermore praising Thee and saying, Holy, Holy, Holy, Lord God of hosts, Heaven and earth are full of Thy glory. Glory be to Thee, O Lord most high." Already, while still in the mid-tide of history, with all its sins and contradictions, the Church is participating in the characteristic work of the redeemed in Heaven. Holiness belongs to eternity.

But, secondly, through worship, too, the Church is

holding aloft a symbol of promise of the consummation of history, when every single activity of mankind
will become an act of worship, of the ascription of
praise to God's glory; when wealth will be produced
more for the glory of God than for human need; when
art will vie with industry for the greater glory of God,
and all life will become an ecstatic awareness of God.
For God's laws belong to eternity.

So every time Christians participate in worship, they
are doing two things—they are at one with the redeemed in the final activity of souls and they are
renewing the promise of the final triumph of God in
glory. "To the glory of Thy Holy Name."

So let us turn to the General Confession, not as a
remote, antiquated, threadbare scripture, but as a
living, relevant document. For here is a profound
utterance of the human soul, of its tragic inner contradictions, its abyss of guilt, its sense of a Holy, Transcendent, Redeeming God. Here, too, is a philosophy
of history, which will strengthen our right arm in the
day of trial, and fortify our souls in an hour of crisis and
judgment. Here, too, is faith's final vision of a trans-
figured humanity, having overcome, having passed
through the Great Tribulation of history, to join with
Christ in His final reign. "Glory be to the Father and
to the Son and to the Holy Ghost; as it was in the
beginning, is now, and ever shall be. Amen."

Indexed 6/04

BX5145A633 D3   CU-Main
c.1
Davies, David Richa/Down, peacock's feathers; stud

3 9371 00037 2318